PRAISE

"As a parent, I wanted to help my son navigate the internship search, but I wasn't sure how. Julia's advice transformed my approach; it wasn't about doing it for him, but equipping him with the strategies to thrive. I felt confident guiding him through the process, and saw him gain more confidence and independence. It was remarkable."

—SHAUNA, PARENT

"If only I had this book when I was 17! This book cuts through the noise and delivers real, actionable strategies that I wish I knew at the start of my career journey. An absolute must-read for any student serious about landing a dream internship."

— ALEX, RECRUITMENT CONSULTANT

"Julia's guidance was a game-changer. From refining my resume to strategizing my job search, her insights were invaluable. She didn't just give advice; she taught me how to negotiate my job offer, and that alone got me an extra $2,000. This book is the playbook every college student needs."

— JACOB, LAW STUDENT

"My son was struggling to get interviews, and I felt lost on how to help him. After consulting with Julia, the transformation was incredible. Her advice on networking and resume building was game-changing, leading directly to two offers. This book is exactly what parents need to give to their students to help navigate this competitive landscape."

— MARCI, PARENT

A Quick Disclaimer

Please note the information contained in this book is provided solely for educational and informational purposes only. While every attempt has been made to provide accurate and up-to-date information, the author makes no guarantees of any kind regarding the specific outcomes or results you may achieve from applying the strategies discussed. The internship and job market is dynamic, and every individual's journey is unique. Readers are advised that the author is not engaging in the rendering of legal, financial, or professional advice. This guide is a resource for career coaching, not a substitute for consultation with qualified professionals.

By reading this book, you agree that you are responsible for your own judgment and actions. The author shall not be held liable for any loss, injury, or damage, direct or indirect, resulting from the use or misuse of the information contained in this work.

ISBN: 979-8-9998642-0-8 (Paperback)

979-8-9998642-1-5 (Ebook)

FROM HI TO HIRED

Your Insider Guide to Internships

JULIA LEVY

CONTENTS

This is where you figure out what you want, how the game is really played, and how to stay sane while doing it.

PART IV: YOU'RE IN! (NOW WHAT?): OFFERS, REJECTION, AND HOW TO BE THE INTERN THEY CAN'T LIVE WITHOUT 192

This is where the real world hits. How to handle offers, bounce back from rejection, and crush your internship from day one.

HELLO STUDENTS

Let's be honest: trying to land an internship can feel like you're putting together a puzzle where half the pieces are missing or a game where the rules are written in a foreign language. Classes, a social life, the relentless anxiety of big career decisions, it's a lot. You're juggling it all.

Feeling lost, you hit the internet. What's waiting for you there?

"Your resume needs a flashy design to stand out." "It's a numbers game, so use AI to mass-apply to 200+ jobs." "Here are five things to lie about during your interview."

Open TikTok or YouTube, and you're flooded with career advice. It's everywhere. Sure, some of it is gold. But much of it? Pure clickbait, engineered for views, not real-world results. The challenge isn't finding advice; it's knowing who and what to trust.

Many online tips focus on 'hacks' and tricks designed to game the system. But as someone who has spent two decades building and improving these systems and leading teams of recruiters, I can tell you that shortcuts often lead to dead ends.

This book isn't about hacks. It's about strategy.

Here's the difference: A hack tries to fool a system you don't understand (think white-text keywords). A strategy? That's about *understanding* the system and the humans running it, so you can present your skills honestly and effectively. Hacks are tempting, yes. But they're fragile. Strategy, on the other hand, is durable. It builds lasting confidence and serves you long after your internship search is over.

Let's look at some common 'quick-fix' myths and compare them to the strategies that actually open doors:

MYTH #1: "YOUR RESUME NEEDS A FLASHY DESIGN …"

- **Strategy:** A flashy resume often fails the Applicant Tracking System (ATS). In this book, I provide advice on how to build a clean, powerful resume that is designed to be read clearly by both software and humans.

MYTH #2: "USE 'TRICKS' LIKE PUTTING KEYWORDS IN WHITE TEXT … "

- **Strategy:** Recruiters and modern systems can easily spot these tricks. I'll teach you the right way to use your skills and accomplishments so you can showcase your capabilities honestly.

MYTH #3: "IT'S A PURE NUMBERS GAME … "

- **Strategy:** A targeted approach is far more effective than a mass application blitz. In the book we'll focus on proactive networking that gets you noticed by the right people.

MY 'WHY' BEHIND WRITING THIS BOOK AND WHAT MAKES IT DIFFERENT

I wasn't born a straight-A student. My report cards were a sea of B's and C's, always with that same maddening teacher's note: "Julia would be an amazing student, if only she applied herself." Sound familiar?

Helping people, that was my clear goal. So, I enrolled as a psychology major at Drexel University, a school renowned for its co-op program. The problem? The program was great ... if you were an engineer or business student. When I looked at the job board, there wasn't a single psychology-related job for me. My 'career prep' class gave me a resume and basic interviewing skills, but it didn't give me a real job search strategy. I had to figure that out on my own.

So, I hustled. Made lists. Sent emails. Made calls. Learned to network when I knew absolutely no one. Through sheer grit, I landed a co-op at one of America's oldest psychiatric hospitals. It was an incredible experience that launched my career, but I had to carve that road myself.

Those early battles caught the attention of my friends. They started asking for help with their resumes, interviews, job searches. That early 'career coaching' for my friends? It became a rewarding career.

I'm Julia Levy. For over two decades, my mission has been simple: connecting talented people with companies that need them. As a Global Talent Acquisition Executive, I've designed the strategies that shape how businesses find and hire top talent. My teams have reviewed millions of resumes and hired hundreds of thousands of people. I've personally evaluated more resumes than I can count and have directly hired hundreds of people in my career. I know precisely what it takes to stand out.

Beyond leading massive hiring teams, I also hold a master's degree in career counseling. This means I can give you not just the 'what,' but the 'why' and the 'how,' helping you build a strategy that's smart, effective, and true to who you are.

WHAT MAKES THIS BOOK DIFFERENT:

Forget the fluff and the 'gurus.' This book isn't from an academic or a motivational speaker who's never been in the trenches. This is your insider's guide, written by someone who's seen both sides of the interview table.

As a Talent Acquisition Executive: I've spent years building recruiting strategies for Fortune 500 companies, sifting through thousands of applications, and helping hiring managers make their decisions. I know exactly what companies want and what sends a resume to the 'no' pile.

As a Career Coach and Counselor: I've helped students navigate job search confusion, overcome rejection, and build confidence. I understand your anxieties and the challenges you face in today's tough job market.

This unique dual perspective allows me to share the 'real' rules of the corporate recruiting game. I'll show you how large companies think and hire, cutting through the noise and bad advice. This isn't just theory; it's battle-tested strategy and empathetic guidance, designed to equip you with the tools you need to land your dream internship.

HOW TO MAXIMIZE YOUR USE OF THIS BOOK

Alright, listen up, future intern! You've got this book in your hands. This isn't some dusty textbook you'll skim for a quiz and forget by next week. This is your personal secret weapon, your backstage pass, your Yoda guiding you through the internship galaxy. But just like a lightsaber, it's only powerful if you know how to wield it.

So, how do you squeeze every drop of intern-landing goodness out of these pages? Don't just read it. *Attack* it. Engage with it. Here's the deal:

- **This Isn't About Hacks: It's About Strategy:** This book isn't about cutting corners; it's about building a solid foundation. You won't find any 'secret hacks' for tricking the system or one-off 'loopholes' to sneak in to an interview. Those might give you a fleeting win, but they're not how lasting success is built. Instead, we're focused on durable strategies, the kind that empower you with genuine understanding and skills. This is about learning the rules of the game and building your capabilities so that you don't need a hack. You'll be playing the game with confidence, integrity, and a skillset that serves you for your entire career, not just this internship search.

- **Don't Just Read,** *do***:** See an activity? Don't just nod your head. Grab a pen, write in the space provided or open a doc, and actually *do* it. This isn't a theory class; it's a workshop. You can't learn to ride a bike by watching someone else do it, right?

- **Highlight, Underline, Annotate:** Make it Your Own Messy Masterpiece: This isn't a library book. Deface it! Circle the 'Insider Insights.' Scribble your questions in the margins. Write down names of companies that pique your interest. The more personal it gets, the more the information sticks.

- **Don't Skip the 'Why':** I'm not just giving you a fish; I'm teaching you how to fish, how to build the fishing pole, and where the best fishing spots are! When I explain *why* a certain strategy works (with the ATS, for example), pay attention. Understanding the 'why' builds your confidence and makes you adaptable when things don't go as planned.

- **Treat it Like a GPS, not a Straightjacket:** This book gives you a roadmap, but your journey is unique. If a chapter sparks an idea or makes you think of a different path, explore it! This isn't about rigid rules, but about smart strategies that you can adapt to your own situations.

- **Revisit, Reread, Reignite:** You're going to hit roadblocks. You're going to get rejected. (It happens to everyone, trust me.) When that doubt creeps in, don't throw the book across the room. Pick it up. Revisit a chapter that speaks to your current challenge. Sometimes, you need to hear the same advice again, but with a fresh perspective.

- **Talk About It:** Don't keep this gold mine to yourself. Discuss the concepts with your friends, your career adviser, even your parents (especially if they're reading our free content for parents). Talking through the strategies will solidify them in your mind and spark new ideas.

This book isn't just about landing *an* internship. It's about landing the *right* internship, and using that experience to launch the career you actually want. This book is your unfair advantage. Now, go get to work!

A NOTE TO PARENTS

First of all, thank you. You've made an investment in your student's future and education. You know the world of work they're stepping into is more competitive than ever. The old rules don't always apply, and you want to give your student the best possible advantage.

This book *is* that advantage. It's the insider's playbook, giving your student the confidence, skills, and strategy to land an internship that will launch their career.

But what about your role? Being your student's biggest supporter is your goal. But how do you help without overstepping? You need to be a coach, not a project manager.

While this book is for your student, we have created companion content for you at hi2hired.com. Information includes:

- Conversation starters for talking about the job search without causing stress.

- A how-to guide to reviewing your student's resume and cover letter, without rewriting it for them.

- Strategies to help students build resilience after facing rejection.

- A clear roadmap for being your child's most effective and supportive coach.

Thank you for being your student's biggest champion. This book will give them the tools to succeed, and the supplemental parent information at hi2hired.com will give you the tools to support them on their journey.

PART I:
FIRST THINGS FIRST:
GETTING YOUR HEAD IN THE GAME

This is where you figure out what you want, how the game is really played, and how to stay sane while doing it.

AN INTERNSHIP ISN'T JUST AN INTERNSHIP

Imagine the world of internships as a theme park, the world's most exciting, in my opinion. (And yes, I'm a fan of Disney, Universal, and Six Flags.) There are incredible, state-of-the-art rides (the amazing jobs and career opportunities). When you arrive, you see long lines of students for all the popular attractions.

Most students get into the main 'Standby Line' by clicking the 'Apply' button online, and they wait, hoping for their turn. A select few are in the 'Lightning Lane,' moving quickly to the front. And you want to know how to get there!

But let's be realistic for a moment. Unlike a theme park where everyone eventually gets on the ride (except on opening weekend for Hagrid's ride at Universal – yes I am still a little bitter all these years later!), employers typically hire one person for each job opportunity or headcount.

So what happens to everyone else in line? This is where a company's values and culture show up. A great company understands: the goal isn't just filling a single seat. It's ensuring every interested person has a positive experience.

For over twenty years, my job was to be the Chief Experience Officer for these parks. My team designed the 'Lightning Lane' to help the most qualified and prepared students get to the front faster. But more importantly, we designed the entire park to be full of other incredible amenities: networking events (the grand parade), skill-building workshops (the interactive exhibits), and transparent communication (the friendly park guides).

My mission? To ensure every candidate left our park feeling valued. Even if their dream ride was unavailable, they'd depart with valuable career 'souvenirs': new professional connections, sharper interviewing skills, and a clear idea of which rides to try next. The goal was for them to leave excited to return. It is important to note that many employers don't have dedicated teams looking at the candidate experience. Some companies have a terrible culture. Are they still worth checking out? In later chapters we will talk through how you can find companies that better align with your aspirations and values.

This book is your all-access guide to getting the most out of your visit. It will show you how to earn that Career Fast Pass for your dream ride, but it will also teach you how to navigate the entire park like a pro. You'll learn how to meet the right people and how to make every interaction a productive one.

This way, your internship search is never a waste of time. It becomes a valuable experience in itself, setting you up for long-term success, no matter which ride you get on first.

THE FOUNDATION FOR YOUR FUTURE

Before we dive into the 'how,' we need to figure out the 'what' and 'why.' At first glance, all internships might look the same. But choosing the right type of internship is the difference between a career-launching opportunity and a summer spent making coffee and copies.

Knowing the difference is crucial. Here's why this should matter to you:

- **Know your 'why.'** Before diving into applications, clarify your core objective. What's the real motive for this internship? Cash, career test run, or just getting your grandparents off your back when they ask what you want to do with your life? Understanding your primary goal helps filter out the noise.

- **Learn actual skills.** This isn't about collecting participation trophies. It's about acquiring capabilities that make you indispensable, not just presentable. Don't just tick a box; become invaluable. Target experiences that will teach you concrete skills, not just give you a line item on your resume.

- **Identify your deal-breakers.** Does it have to be paid? Does it need to be in a specific city? Does it have to be remote? Figuring out your non-negotiables from the start will save you a lot of time and frustration.

- **Play the long game.** The ultimate goal of an internship isn't just the internship itself, it's getting the full-time job offer, setting you up for graduate school or helping you rule out a career path that didn't feel quite right when you tried it on.

WHAT EXACTLY ARE WE TALKING ABOUT, ANYWAY?

Let's clear up some confusion. People throw around terms like 'internship' and 'summer job' like they're the same thing. They are not. Here's the insider's breakdown:

- **Internship:** This is your career test drive. A structured, short-term (typically 8-12 weeks) immersion in a specific field or company. For big companies, it's the primary recruiting tool for entry-level full-time hires. They are 'test-driving' you, too.

- **Summer job:** Think of this as earning Robux / V-Bucks. It's primarily about getting a paycheck. You'll gain valuable skills such as responsibility and teamwork at your hospitality, retail or food service job, but it's not designed to be a direct launchpad into a specific corporate career.

- **Entry-Level job:** This is buying the car. Your full-time gig after graduation. And a great internship is the single best way to land it.

⚙ ACTIVITY: LET'S FIND YOUR 'WHY': YOUR INTERNSHIP COMPASS

This isn't a test, and there are no wrong answers. This is a quick gut check to figure out what you *really* want, so you can start looking in the right places.

Step 1: Your Gut Reaction: In one sentence, what do you hope an internship will do for you right now? (Seriously, no overthinking this!)

_____

_____

_____

Step 2: What's Your Real Motivation? Beyond just 'getting experience,' what are your **top three personal goals** for an internship? Circle or highlight your top three from the list below, or add your own.

- Earn money

- Build a specific technical skill (like coding, financial modeling, etc.)

- Explore a career path I'm curious about

- Grow my professional network

- Earn required credit for school

- Get the name of a prestigious company on my resume

- Secure a full-time job offer from this company

- (Your own goal): _____

Step 3: What You've Already Done (Your Experience Inventory): List any jobs, volunteer work, or big projects you've done during school. Decide if it was a 'Test Drive,' 'Fuel Money,' or 'Full-Time Gig.' What's the #1 skill you learned from each?

- **Experience 1:** _____

  - Type:

  - #1 Skill Learned:

- **Experience 2:** _____

  - Type:

  - #1 Skill Learned:

- **Experience 3:** _____

  - Type:

  - #1 Skill Learned:

- **Experience 4:** _____

  - Type:

  - #1 Skill Learned:

Step 4: Your #1 Deal-Breaker: If you could only guarantee **one thing** from your next internship for it to be a success, what would it be? (e.g., "It MUST be paid," "It MUST be in the tech industry," "It MUST offer direct mentorship.") This is your non-negotiable.

My non-negotiable is: _____

💡 INSIDER INSIGHT

I've seen it a thousand times. A student lands an internship at 'Big Famous Company A' and thinks they've hit the jackpot. They spend their summer fetching coffee, making spreadsheets no one ever looks at, and getting lost in the corporate labyrinth. Impressive name on the resume, sure, but their skills? Still stuck on 'beginner' mode. Then there's the other student, who maybe took a chance on 'Mid-Size Company B' that no one's heard of outside their industry. That kid ends up building something real, presenting to the actual CEO, and gets a job offer they're genuinely excited about. The moral of the story? Don't chase the logo. Chase the learning. Your future self will thank you.

THE BOTTOM LINE

Let's do a quick gut check. Do you feel the shift?

Instead of just blindly applying for jobs, you now have a new mindset. You understand that you're not just trying to get on one ride, but to have a successful day at the park. You know that there's a 'Standby Line' and a 'Lightning Lane,' and you're going to learn your way into the faster one.

Most importantly, you've started to define what a 'win' looks like for you personally.

Hold onto that feeling. Now that you know your 'why,' let's go find your 'what.' Up next in Chapter 2, we'll break down the different kinds of internships you'll find out there.

DECODING INTERNSHIPS: UNDERSTANDING THE POSSIBILITIES

Now that you've figured out *why* you're on this journey, let's explore the 'what.' It helps to think of the world of internships as a massive park map laid out in front of you.

This map reveals the amusement park's diverse themed lands: 'The Land of Big Tech,' 'Non-Profit World,' and 'Startup City.' Each land offers unique rides and experiences, and understanding this park map is your next strategic move to choose the perfect adventure.

This chapter is your guide. I'm going to break down the main categories of internships so you can understand what's out there and start matching the right opportunities to the personal goals you just set.

THE MANY FACES OF AN INTERNSHIP: A CATEGORIZED GUIDE

An internship isn't a single, uniform experience; it's a diverse landscape with opportunities that vary wildly based on their purpose, structure, and the benefits they offer. To truly make an informed decision and target roles that align with your aspirations, it's essential to understand these fundamental distinctions. Let's explore the various categories of internships you'll encounter on your journey.

BY COMPENSATION

You want to know about money? Let's talk about the cold, hard facts of internship compensation. This isn't just about cash; it's about what a company values and what you're truly getting in to.

- **Paid Internships:**

  o **What they are:** These roles pay you, usually an hourly wage (typically $18 - $30). You'll find them at medium to large corporations in sectors like tech, consulting, finance, and engineering. They are often the most in-demand opportunities.

  o **The Perks:** Financial independence is the biggest benefit. Paid internships tend to be highly structured, with clear responsibilities and strong mentorship because the company is making a direct investment in you. These companies typically have a goal to hire 50% - 70% of their former interns upon graduation.

  o **Things to Consider:** The catch? Everyone wants one. Competition is cutthroat, and sometimes, the work itself can feel less impactful, more like a cog in a massive machine.

- **Unpaid Internships:**

  o **What they are:** These roles offer experience without direct pay, though you can often earn academic credit. They are common in nonprofits, the arts, government, and some startups where budgets are tight.

  o **The Perks:** They provide real-world experience, a chance to build your portfolio, and opportunity to prove your passion.

  o **Things to Consider:** It's a career test-drive, but only if you can afford the gas. It's crucial to ensure the role offers structured learning and mentorship so that you are gaining valuable skills, not just doing free administrative work.

- **Stipend-Based Internships:**

  o **What they are:** A middle ground where you receive a fixed sum of money (a stipend) to help offset costs like housing, food, or transportation. It's not an hourly wage.

  o **The Perks:** The stipend provides some financial breathing room and is a sign that the organization values your contribution, even if it can't afford to pay you an actual salary.

  o **Things to Consider:** A stipend may not cover all of your expenses, so you'll need to budget carefully before accepting the role.

BY LOCATION AND STRUCTURE

Where and how you work fundamentally shapes your experience.

- **On-Site Internships:** This is the traditional model where you work at the company's office. It's the best way to be fully immersed in the company culture, benefit from spontaneous conversations, and build face-to-face relationships with mentors and teammates. However, it may require you to commute or relocate.

- **Remote Internships:** You work from anywhere outside the company office, using digital tools to collaborate. This offers maximum flexibility as you can work for a company located anywhere in the world. This path demands strong self-discipline, time management, and proactive communication. However, it can be limiting with regard to face-to-face networking and relationship building.

- **Hybrid Internships:** A blend of both on-site and remote work. This model can provide the 'best of both worlds': the structure and social connection of the office, plus the flexibility and autonomy of working from anywhere.

BY DURATION AND INTENSITY

The time commitment for an internship can vary significantly.

- **Summer Internships:** The most common format. These are typically full time (40 hours / week) for 10-12 weeks over the summer. They offer an immersive, focused experience and are a primary pipeline for full-time hiring at many companies.

- **Semester / Academic Year Internships:** These are part-time roles you hold during the fall or spring semester alongside your classes. They require excellent time management but allow you to apply classroom learning in real-time.

- **Cooperative Education (Co-ops):** Longer, more intensive programs, often lasting six months or more and integrated into your university's curriculum. They provide much deeper, hands-on experience and are almost always paid.

- **Externships and Micro-Internships:** These are short-term, focused experiences. An **externship** is a brief job-shadowing opportunity (a few days to a week). A **micro-internship** is a short-term, paid project (usually 10-40 hours total). Both are excellent ways to explore a career or build a specific skill without a long commitment.

BY ACADEMIC AFFILIATION

Finally, consider how an internship connects to your degree.

- **For-Credit Internships:** These are formally recognized by your university and count toward your graduation requirements. They involve specific learning objectives and oversight from a faculty member.

- **Non-Credit Internships:** These are pursued purely for the professional experience and do not have any formal connection to your academic program.

⚙ ACTIVITY: CREATING YOUR INTERNSHIP TARGET PROFILE

Okay, we've looked at the map. Now it's time to design *your* perfect path. In the last chapter, you found your 'why.' Now we're going to build a practical filter to make your search way more effective. This isn't a test—it's your personal game plan.

STEP 1: THE DEAL-BREAKERS

Let's start with the big stuff. Based on your 'Internship Compass,' answer these questions with your preferences.

- **The Money:** What's your absolute minimum? (e.g., "Must be paid hourly," "I'd be satisfied with a stipend to cover my travel expenses," "I can do unpaid if I get credit.")

- **The Location:** Where do you need to be? (e.g., "Must be remote," "Hybrid in the NYC area," "I'm willing to relocate for the summer.")

- **The Time:** How much can you realistically commit? (e.g., "Full-time for the summer only," "15 hours / week during the fall semester.")

STEP 2: YOUR 'TOP 5' VALUES

You can't have everything in every experience, so what do you value most? Review the list below, aligning them to your personal values and **choose your top five.** These are the features you'll look for to know if an internship is a great fit.

- Learning & Skill Building

- Impact / Meaningful Work

- Strong Mentorship

- Future Opportunity (potential for a full-time job)

- Great Team / Social Connection

- Innovation / Creativity

- Autonomy / Independence

- Work-Life Balance

- Diversity & Inclusion

- (Your Own Value): _____

STEP 3: YOUR INTERNSHIP FOCUS STATEMENT

Now, put it all together. Write one clear sentence that declares what you're looking for. This is your mission statement for the hunt.

> **Example:** "My focus is on finding a **paid, remote** summer internship in marketing where I can get **strong mentorship** and build my **creative skills**."

Write your focus statement here:

My focus is on: _____

_____

_____

💡INSIDER INSIGHT

I once coached a student named Alex who at first aimed for high-paying finance internships because that's what he thought he was 'supposed' to do. But after doing this activity, he discovered that his top values were actually 'Impact' and 'Strong Mentorship.' He pivoted his search, found a paid role at a B-Corp (a for-profit company with a social mission), and had an amazing experience that led to a full-time offer. Knowing what you truly want can be your most powerful tool.

THE BOTTOM LINE

No more guessing. You now have a clear picture of the internship landscape and, more importantly, where you want to go. This isn't just about knowing what's out there; it's about knowing what's right for you. That focused aim? That's your new secret weapon. It means you stop wasting time on opportunities that are dead ends and start pouring all your energy into the ones that actually matter.

A GUIDE FOR INTERNATIONAL STUDENTS: NAVIGATING VISAS, SPONSORSHIP, AND YOUR SECRET WEAPON

As an international student seeking a U.S. internship, you're playing the game on 'hard mode.' You're not just navigating a new professional culture; you're also wrestling with a complex web of visas, work authorizations, and sponsorship questions that can feel overwhelming.

It is harder for you. But let me be clear: it is absolutely not impossible. In fact, your international background, the very thing that creates these hurdles, is also your unique professional advantage.

As a recruiter, I've hired hundreds of incredible international students. The ones who succeeded were the ones who understood the system, were relentlessly proactive, and knew how to frame their global perspective as a massive competitive advantage. This chapter is your playbook for doing exactly that.

Disclaimer: I am a recruiting expert, not an immigration attorney. The information here is for guidance and context. Your absolute #1 resource for all visa and work authorization questions is your university's International Student

Services (ISS) office or an attorney. They are the experts. Make an appointment with them now.

DECODING THE ALPHABET SOUP: CPT, OPT, AND SPONSORSHIP

Let's demystify the terms you'll hear constantly.

- **CPT (Curricular Practical Training):** Think of this as your internship work permit while you're still a student. It allows you to work in a role that is an integral part of your academic curriculum. Your ISS office has to approve it, and it's typically used for internships during the summer or part-time during the school year.

- **OPT (Optional Practical Training):** This is your work permit for after you graduate. It allows you to work for 12 months in a job directly related to your major. For students with STEM degrees (Science, Technology, Engineering, and Math), you may be eligible for a 24-month extension, for a total of 36 months of OPT.

- **Sponsorship (The H-1B Visa):** This is the long-term goal for many. It's a work visa that allows a U.S. company to employ a foreign professional for several years. It's a complex, expensive, and lottery-based process for the employer.

For your internship, you will almost always be using CPT. This is a huge advantage, because it means the company does not need to 'sponsor' you for the internship itself.

THE SPONSORSHIP QUESTION: HOW TO ANSWER WITH CONFIDENCE

Almost every online application will hit you with this: "Will you now or in the future require sponsorship for employment visa status (e.g., H-1B visa status)?" It's a tricky one. Your gut might scream 'No!' to avoid being filtered. Don't. Honesty is critical; a dishonest answer can cost you the opportunity entirely.

- **The Correct Answer is 'Yes.'** If you hope to work in the U.S. after graduation using OPT and eventually need an H-1B visa, the truthful answer is 'Yes.'

- **Why it Matters:** Companies ask this for long-term planning. They want to know if they will need to go through the sponsorship process for you if they decide to hire you full-time after your internship.

- **How to Frame it:** In your cover letter or interviews, you can proactively clarify your situation. "Just to be clear, while I will require sponsorship for full-time employment in the future, I am fully authorized to work in the U.S. for this internship under my F-1 visa's CPT."

This shows you understand the process and are on top of your own work authorization, which is a very professional and reassuring signal to a recruiter.

HUNTING FOR SPONSORSHIP-FRIENDLY COMPANIES

The reality is that not all companies sponsor international students for full-time roles. Smaller companies and startups often don't have the resources or legal expertise. Your search needs to be targeted.

- **Target Large, Multinational Corporations:** Big companies (like the ones in the Fortune 500) are your best bet. They have experienced immigration law teams, established processes for hiring international talent, and see your global perspective as an asset.

- **Use Your University's Resources:** Your ISS office and Career Center often have lists of companies that have hired international students from your school in the past. This is a goldmine.

- **Leverage Online Databases:** Websites like MyVisaJobs.com and Hired.com allow you to search for companies that have sponsored H-1B visas in the past. This is powerful data for building your target list.

- **The Alumni Secret Weapon:** Use LinkedIn to find other international alumni from your university who are now working in the U.S. They have successfully navigated this exact path. They are your most valuable source of advice and potential referrals.

INSIDER INSIGHT: THE INTERNSHIP IS THE REAL INTERVIEW FOR A FULL-TIME JOB

Here is one of the most important insider secrets for international students: many large companies will only hire international students for full-time positions if they have successfully completed an internship with them first. Why? Because sponsoring an H-1B visa is an expensive and lengthy legal commitment for a company. It's a big investment. They are much more willing to make that investment in a 'known quantity,' someone who has already spent 10 weeks working with their team, has proven their skills, and has shown they are a great cultural fit. The internship is a 10-week, low-risk interview for the company. This should change your entire mindset. For you, the internship isn't just about getting experience; it is the primary pathway to getting a full-time, sponsored job in the U.S. This makes every piece of advice in this book from tailoring your resume to acing your projects even more critical.

YOUR GLOBAL BACKGROUND IS A SUPERPOWER

Don't ever let the visa process make you feel like your background is a liability. It is your single greatest strength. In a global economy, companies are desperate for employees who bring a diverse perspective. You just need to learn how to sell it.

- **You're Multilingual:** This isn't just a 'nice-to-have'; it's a powerful business skill.

- **You're Cross-Culturally Adept:** You have firsthand experience navigating different cultural norms, which is invaluable for any company that works with international clients or teams.

- **You're Adaptable and Resilient:** You've already navigated the massive challenge of moving to and studying in a new country. This proves you are adaptable, independent, and can thrive in unfamiliar situations.

'Before and After' Resume Framing:

- **Before:** A simple 'Languages' section listing 'Fluent in Mandarin.'
- **After:**

  o A 'Skills' section that lists 'Languages: Fluent in Mandarin, Proficient in English.'

  o A bullet point under a project that says: "Presented project findings to a diverse team, leveraging cross-cultural communication skills to ensure clarity and alignment."

💡 INSIDER INSIGHT: THE INTERN WHO CONNECTED THE DOTS

I once interviewed an international student for a supply chain internship. When I asked about his greatest strength, he didn't just say he was a hard worker. He said, "My experience navigating the logistics of moving my life from India to the U.S. has given me a real-world understanding of global supply chains. I've personally dealt with customs, shipping delays, and cross-cultural communication challenges. I know how to solve those problems because I've lived them." He had brilliantly connected his personal life experience to our business needs. We offered him the internship.

⚙ ACTIVITY: YOUR INTERNATIONAL STUDENT STRATEGY PLAN

STEP 1: MEET YOUR ADVISER:

Make an appointment with your university's ISS office this month. Write down three specific questions you will ask them about CPT and your internship search.

STEP 2: BUILD YOUR TARGET LIST:

Using the strategies in this chapter, identify five large, multinational companies in your target industry that have a history of hiring international students.

STEP 3: FRAME YOUR SUPERPOWER:

Write one powerful bullet point for your resume that transforms your international background into a professional skill.

INSIDER INSIGHT: BE STRATEGIC

Applying to every open internship you see? That's a common mistake, especially among international students. It feels like you're increasing your chances, but it actually works against you. Campus recruiting teams value focused, strategic applications. They're more likely to consider you for suitable roles if your initial application shows clear intent, rather than a scattershot approach.

THE BOTTOM LINE

As an international student, your internship quest comes with extra paper-work, extra rules, and sometimes, extra headaches. It's like playing the game on expert mode from the get-go. But here's the thing: the very fact that you're even attempting this proves you're resourceful, adaptable, and have grit. These aren't just personality traits; they're high-demand professional skills. By under-standing the system, being proactive, and confidently framing your global experience as the superpower it is, you won't just be a great candidate in spite of your background; you'll be a great candidate *because* of it.

WELCOME TO THE GAME: HOW RECRUITING REALLY WORKS

To win the game, you first need to understand how it's played.

Let's talk about what actually happens when you hit that 'Apply' button.

When you hit 'Apply' at a major company, you're not just sending a resume. You're pressing 'Start' on a massive, complex video game with its own rules, levels, and key players. Think of this chapter as your game manual. We're pulling back the curtain to give you the complete world map, a guide to the characters you'll meet on your quest, and the strategies you need to master to win.

THE SCALE OF THE GAME: IT'S BIGGER THAN YOU THINK

Let's talk about real numbers. A popular summer internship program at one of my former companies received thousands of applications for fewer than 100 spots. It was intensely competitive because we were very intentional about it: our goal was to hire at least 60% of our interns for full-time roles after graduation.

For us, the internship program wasn't just about getting extra help for the summer; it was an extended, high-stakes interview for the future of our company. This is why large employers don't just have a generic 'HR' department. They have dedicated Recruiting or Talent Acquisition (TA) teams. Think of them as the game designers who are specialists in finding the right talent. These teams are often broken down into even more specialized groups.

MEET THE PLAYERS: WHO YOU'LL ENCOUNTER ON YOUR QUEST

You'll interact with a few different people during your internship search. Knowing who they are and what they care about is a huge advantage.

- **The Campus Recruiter (Your First Ally):** This is your most important contact. Their entire job revolves around finding and hiring students like you. They understand your academic calendar, they know you're not a seasoned pro, and they're the first eyes on your resume. Think of them as the friendly NPC (non-player character) who hands you the first map and a crucial tip. Your goal? Build a great relationship.

- **The Hiring Manager (The Level Boss):** This is the person you will actually work for. They make the final hiring decision. They aren't just looking for a good student; they are looking for a problem-solver who can add real value to the team.

- **The Interview Panel (The Multi-Stage Boss Battle):** For some roles, you'll meet with a group of people. Each person is there to test a different skill or competency. One might focus on your technical knowledge, another on your teamwork, and another on your ability to fit in with the company's culture.

- **Specialty Recruiters:** You might also encounter recruiters who specialize in certain areas. **Corporate Recruiters** handle experienced hires but might help with hard-to-fill intern roles. **Military** and **Diversity Recruiters** focus on building a diverse talent pipeline and partner with student groups. For highly technical roles, **Specialty Recruiters** with deep industry knowledge are brought in.

- **The Coordinator:** Many TA teams have coordinators or specialists that help with the administrative side of the process. This may be the person scheduling your interviews or assisting with the administration of a Summer Internship Program.

INSIDER INSIGHT: A CAMPUS RECRUITER'S DAY IN THE LIFE (DURING PEAK SEASON)

Picture this: it's peak recruiting season, and my team of campus recruiters is running at full speed. Their day could start at 7 a.m., setting up for a career fair hours away from home. They'll spend the day talking to hundreds of students, collecting resumes, and making quick notes on the most promising candidates. In the afternoon, they might have back-to-back phone screens, and then they'll hop on a flight to the next university. When they're not on the road, they're sorting through hundreds of online applications, coordinating with hiring managers, and making decisions that shape the future of the company. They are incredibly busy, which is why making a clear, positive, and memorable impression is so important.

WHERE THE GAME IS PLAYED: HOW COMPANIES FIND YOU

Big companies don't just post a job and hope for the best. They go hunting for talent in specific places.

- **Campus Career Fairs:** These aren't just for grabbing free pens and swag. This is a company's chance to scout talent in person. A great conversation at a career fair can be the 'power-up' that gets your resume to the top of the pile. Make sure to sign up and check in ahead of time. Come prepared with a concise pitch and ask smart questions that show you've done your research.

- **University Partnerships & 'Core Schools':** My recruiting teams always had 'core schools' we focused on. With a limited budget, we had to be strategic about where we spent our time. We built deep relationships with universities that had strong programs in the fields we hired for most.

- **Insider Tip (and this is a big one):** Just because your school isn't a 'core school' does not mean you can't get hired. It just means you have to be more proactive. We reviewed every single online application, regardless of the school. Your online application and LinkedIn profile become your primary introduction, so they need to be flawless. Don't ever count yourself out.

- **Online Platforms (LinkedIn, Handshake, etc.):** Companies use these tools, but they don't just sit back and wait. Recruiters are actively searching these platforms for students with the right skills. This is why having a great, keyword-optimized LinkedIn profile (which we'll cover later) is so important.

- **Referrals (the Ultimate Power-Up):** This is the most powerful way to get your foot in the door. Think of it like finding a rare item that gives your character a massive boost. A referral from a current employee can often move your application straight past the initial screening and directly to the recruiting team. It's a huge advantage that helps you bypass the early levels of the game. Many companies even reward employees for referring great candidates because those hires tend to perform well and stay longer.

THE GAME CLOCK: WHEN TO APPLY

Understanding the campus recruiting calendar is critical. You can be the most qualified student in the world, but if you apply too late, it won't matter.

- **Peak Season (The Main Event): Fall (September–November)** is the primary recruiting season for summer internships for the following year. Yes, you read that right. You apply almost a year in advance for the most competitive roles in fields like finance, consulting, and tech.

- **Second Wave (Spring Season):** Some companies continue to recruit in the **spring (January–March)**, but the pool of available spots is much smaller.

- **The Golden Rule: APPLY EARLY.** I cannot stress this enough. Most companies review applications on a rolling basis. The sooner you apply, the better your chances. Waiting until the deadline is one of the biggest mistakes you can make.

⚙ ACTIVITY: SCOUTING THE GAME BOARD

Choose one or two companies where you'd love to intern. Now, let's do some reconnaissance. Use their career pages, LinkedIn, and your university's career site to answer these questions:

STEP 1: WHO ARE THE PLAYERS?

Can you find any 'Campus Recruiters' for that company on LinkedIn? Try searching for "Campus Recruiter at [Company Name]." Other good search terms are "University Relations at [Company Name]." or "Early Careers at [Company Name]." If you find one, save their profile, add them to your network, and connect with them. This person is a key contact.

STEP 2: WHAT'S THEIR STRATEGY?

How does this company find interns? Do they talk about their university partnerships? Do they attend career fairs at your school?

STEP 3: DO YOU HAVE A 'POWER-UP'?

Do you know anyone (family, friends, alumni) who works there? If so, you have a potential referral.

STEP 4: WHAT'S THE TIMELINE?

Is there any information on this company's career site about when they open applications for summer internships? Note the dates.

💡INSIDER INSIGHT: THE INTERESTED CANDIDATE

I remember a student at a career fair a few years ago who didn't just hand me a resume, he struck up a real conversation about a recent tech project our company had announced. He asked smart questions about the challenges involved and connected that to a personal project he'd worked on, demonstrating his problem-solving skills without me even asking. That level of genuine curiosity and proactive storytelling made him stand out immediately. I fast-tracked his resume, and he joined us as an intern the following summer.

THE BOTTOM LINE

The corporate recruiting world isn't a mystery; it's a system. Now that you understand the players, the timing, and the strategies involved, you're no longer just a passive applicant. You're an informed player who knows how the game works. Companies see internships as more than just short-term help; they're an extended interview for a full-time role. This mindset should shift how you approach every part of the process.

In the next chapter, we'll break down the first gatekeeper of this entire process: the Applicant Tracking System (ATS). You'll learn how to make sure your application doesn't just disappear, but actually reaches human eyes.

DECODING THE DIGITAL GATEKEEPER: THE APPLICANT TRACKING SYSTEM (ATS)

Game manual read. World, players, and rules understood. Your quest awaits. But before facing the hiring manager, you've got one locked gate: the Applicant Tracking System (ATS).

It's not a monster you have to fight; it's a high-tech lock. It's not personal; it's a machine. Every major employer uses an ATS to manage the tens of thousands to millions of applications they receive. This chapter is about giving you the right set of keys (keywords) and the proper technique (formatting) to open that gate smoothly and get inside where the real challenges await.

HOW ATS WORKS: THE LOCK'S MECHANISM

At its core, an ATS is part database, part search engine, and increasingly, part AI assistant. When you upload your resume, the system 'parses' your document. Imagine the parser as a robot that 'reads' your resume by stripping away all the visual formatting and converting it into a simple text file. It then tries to identify and categorize the information: this block of text is 'Contact Info,' this block is 'Work Experience,' and this block is a 'Skill.' It then organizes the data into a searchable profile for the recruiter. What they can't do is interpret fancy graphics and images into data that is able to be stored or searched.

After you apply, your resume is first scanned by the ATS to see how well it lines up with the job's needs. Recruiters rely on the ATS to manage the huge volume of applications. They might review current employees or referred candidates first, then move to external applicants who clearly meet the required skills. If your application prominently displays the necessary qualifications, it's far more likely to get a human look. Increasingly, companies are using AI within their ATS to identify highly qualified candidates (based on the job posting requirements) and even fast-track them in the process.

The real power and challenge of an ATS is in the search function. Recruiters type in keywords pulled straight from the job description. The ATS then scans every submitted resume for these terms. In some cases, it scores or ranks resumes based on how closely they match. ATS looks at whether the right keywords appear, how often they show up, and sometimes even where they appear in relation to each other. If your resume doesn't include the right keywords or is formatted in a way the ATS can't easily read, you risk being filtered out long before an actual human recruiter lays eyes on your application.

💡 **INSIDER INSIGHT: THE 'NEAR MISS' RESUME**

I've seen many resumes from brilliant, qualified candidates that were overlooked simply because a fancy font or a graphic confused the ATS, leaving their application incomplete and invisible to the recruiter. Your attention to ATS-friendly formatting can mean the difference between getting noticed or disappearing into a black hole.

THE NEXT LEVEL: AI SCREENING AND YOUR CHOICE TO OPT-IN

While traditional ATS focuses on keywords, the game is changing. Many companies are now integrating Artificial Intelligence directly into their systems, creating a more sophisticated, and sometimes optional, screening process.

FROM FILING CABINET TO AI MATCHMAKER

This transforms the system from a simple keyword-matching tool into an intelligent recruiting assistant. Instead of just searching for words, AI-powered ATS can:

- **Analyze Context:** The AI can understand the context of your skills and experiences, going beyond just matching keywords to assess the quality and relevance of your background.

- **Identify High-Potential Candidates:** Some AI models can analyze the profiles of a company's current top performers and then search the applicant pool for candidates with similar skills, career trajectories, and attributes.

- **Fast-Track Applications:** Based on this deeper analysis, the system can score or rank applicants, flagging high-potential candidates and fast-tracking their resumes directly to a human recruiter's screen.

THE NEW CHOICE: OPTING IN OR OUT OF AI SCREENING

As AI becomes more integrated, a new feature is emerging: giving candidates a choice. When you apply, you may be asked if you consent to have your application reviewed using AI. This is a critical strategic decision.

- **Choosing to 'Opt-In'** means you are giving the company permission to use its AI tools to analyze your entire application. If your skills and experience are a strong match, the AI is designed to recognize this and can significantly accelerate your candidacy. It acts as your advocate, ensuring your profile gets a priority review.

- **Choosing to 'Opt-Out'** means your application will bypass the advanced AI analysis and follow a more traditional workflow. If you have a non-traditional background or believe your unique story is best understood by a person, opting out requires a human to make the initial judgment call. However, your resume will likely be filtered using basic keyword searches and may take longer to be reviewed manually.

MAKING YOUR STRATEGIC DECISION

There is no single right answer; the choice depends on your strategy.

- **Consider Opting in if:** You have a straightforward background that aligns well with the job's stated qualifications and you want the best chance to have your application seen quickly.

- **Consider Opting out if:** You have a unique career path or a 'story' that requires human interpretation, and you are willing to potentially wait longer in the review process to get that human touch.

ATS-FRIENDLY FORMATTING: YOUR GUIDE

The Do's: Your Green Light to Getting Seen

- **Simple, Clean Layout:** Think single column, chronological. The ATS is like a robot, not a graphic designer. It reads top to bottom. Make it easy.

- **Standard Fonts:** Stick to the classics: Arial, Calibri, or Times New Roman. Anything else turns your stellar skills into digital gibberish.

- **Conventional Headings:** 'Experience,' 'Education,' and 'Skills.' Period. The ATS knows these. 'My Journey' just confuses the machine.

- **Simple Bullets:** Solid circles or squares. No fancy arrows or complex symbols. Don't give the parser a reason to misinterpret your genius.

- **Special Characters:** Avoid special characters, as they can interfere with Applicant Tracking Systems (ATS) and prevent your resume from being accurately parsed.

- **Standard File Types:** PDF is usually your safest bet. But if the posting says .docx, give them .docx. Always follow instructions.

- **Clear File Naming:** 'Resume.pdf'? Amateur hour. Make it 'FirstNameLastName_Company_Position.pdf.' Help the recruiter find you. It will score you some bonus points!

THE DON'TS: RED FLAGS THAT KILL YOUR CHANCES

- **No Graphics or Images:** Logos, photos, or bar graphs? Instant death. The ATS can't read them. Your brilliant design just became a black hole.

- **No Critical Info in Headers or Footers:** Your name and contact details belong in the main body. Some systems ignore headers. Don't risk it.

- **No Tables or Columns:** This is a trap. Columns scramble your info, making your experience section read like nonsense. The machine won't get it.

- **No Complex Formatting:** Bright colors, intricate borders, or text boxes. They disrupt the parsing. Keep it clean, keep it clear.

YOUR KEYWORD STRATEGY: SPEAKING THE SYSTEM'S LANGUAGE

This is possibly the most crucial part of optimizing for an ATS: aligning your resume's language with the job description. The goal is simple: speak the system's language so you get seen by the digital gatekeeper.

- **Read Every Line, Strategically:** Carefully read the job description line by line. Highlight or jot down all the important skills, responsibilities, tools, technologies, and qualifications the employer lists. Pay special attention to any repeated words or phrases as these are likely key to what the company is looking for in a prospective new hire.

- **Prioritize Hard Skills:** These are the easiest for an ATS to match. Look for keywords like Python, SQL, Salesforce, Data Analysis, or Project Management. Ensure these appear in your resume, ideally within your skills section and integrated naturally into your experience descriptions.

- **Include Soft Skills, too:** Although harder for an ATS to weigh, soft skills like Communication, Teamwork, Problem-Solving, and Leadership are often included in searches. Weave these into your experience where they genuinely fit.

- **Use Exact Phrases Thoughtfully:** If the posting says 'Customer Relationship Management (CRM),' include both the full term and the acronym if you have that experience. The system might be searching for either.

- **Tailor for Each Role:** There is no universal version of your resume that works for every job. For ATS purposes, customize it for every application so your wording matches the specific keywords in each posting. This is essential to ensure you pass the initial filter.

YOUR NEW AI CO-PILOT: USING AI AS A STRATEGIC TOOL (AND WHAT TO AVOID)

Let's talk about AI. You're probably already using platforms like ChatGPT or Gemini, powerful tools that are here to stay. The real question isn't if you'll use AI in your internship search, but how: as a strategic co-pilot, or a lazy autopilot?

The difference is everything.

The autopilot student uses an AI to apply to 100 random internships in a few minutes or copies and pastes a generic, AI-written cover letter that a recruiter can spot from a mile away. The co-pilot student uses AI to brainstorm ideas on which internship opportunities align best with their goals, polishes their own writing, and gets a powerful first draft to infuse with their unique voice and experiences.

This chapter is your guide to being a smart co-pilot.

THE GOLDEN RULE OF AI: NEVER JUST COPY AND PASTE

AI is an incredible assistant, but it's a terrible impersonator. It doesn't know your stories, your voice, or your unique passions. Its output is, by definition, generic. A recruiter who reads a cover letter that says, "I am a highly motivated and results-oriented individual ... " immediately knows it was written by a robot.

Your job is to take the AI's output and make it yours. Use it as a starting point, a brainstorm partner, or an editor, but not as a final product.

I used AI as a helper in writing this book. It gave me some chapter ideas I had not thought of, suggested a different chapter organization to improve flow, provided ideas for the book title, did some grammatical checks, and helped me write up a marketing plan for book launch.

💡 INSIDER INSIGHT: THE RISE OF THE AI CLONE

As a recruiter, my team and I started noticing a pattern. We'd get waves of applicants who are not qualified for jobs with resumes and cover letters that all sounded eerily similar. They used the same buzzwords, the same sentence structures, and had the same bland, overly formal tone. These were the 'AI clones.' While the grammar was perfect, they had zero personality and showed no genuine interest in our company. They were the easiest applications to reject. The candidates who used AI to enhance their own unique story, to make their ideas clearer and more concise, were the ones who stood out.

THE 'CO-PILOT' PLAYBOOK: USING AI AT EVERY STAGE

Think of AI as a smart but uncreative assistant. You have to provide the strategy and the raw material (your experiences). Let's break down how to use it strategically for your internship search.

PHASE 1: SELF-ASSESSMENT & EXPLORATION (BEFORE YOU EVEN BEGIN)

Before you can find the right internship, you need to understand yourself. AI can be a great sounding board.

- **Identifying Your Skills:** Stuck on what your skills even are? Feed AI your experiences. Prompt: "Act as a career coach. I am a college student. My experiences include being a barista, volunteering for a campus club's social media, and a major class project on the history of trade routes. Based on this, what are 10 transferable skills I likely have?"

- **Exploring Career Paths:** Not sure what you can do with your major? Prompt: "I am a sociology major who is interested in technology and creative work. What are five potential internship roles or career paths that could combine these interests?"

PHASE 2: RESEARCH & TARGETING (FINDING YOUR COMPANIES)

AI is a powerful research assistant that can save you hours of work.

- **Finding Companies That Match Your Values:** Prompt: "I am looking for an internship in the renewable energy sector. My top values are innovation and a strong company culture. What are 10 companies in this industry known for having a great culture for interns? Please provide a brief reason for each."

- **Summarizing Complex Information:** Found a long annual report or a dense article about a target company? Prompt: "Summarize the key takeaways from this article about [company name]'s Q3 earnings report in three bullet points, focusing on information relevant to a potential marketing intern."

PHASE 3: CRAFTING YOUR APPLICATION MATERIALS

This is where most students use AI, but you'll do it in a smarter way.

- **For Your Resume:** Prompt: "Act as a career coach. I was a 'Camp Counselor.' My duties were supervising 15 kids, planning daily activities, and communicating with parents. Help me write three professional, quantified resume bullet points for a 'Project Management' internship that highlight transferable skills like leadership, organization, and communication."

- **For Your Cover Letter:** Prompt: "Help me brainstorm an opening paragraph for a cover letter. I am applying for a Software Engineering internship at Google. I am a computer science student, and I'm passionate about their work on AI accessibility tools. Draft a compelling hook that connects my passion to Google's specific work and makes me sound like an enthusiastic but professional student."

- **For Your LinkedIn Headline:** Prompt: "I am a history major at [your university]. My key skills are research, writing, and critical thinking. I am seeking an internship in the 'Market Research' industry. Generate three compelling and keyword-rich LinkedIn headline options under 220 characters that a recruiter would be likely to search for."

PHASE 4: PREPARING FOR THE INTERVIEW

AI can be your personal interview prep coach, available 24/7.

- **Generating Practice Questions:** Prompt: "I have an upcoming behavioral interview for a 'Data Analyst Internship' at a major tech company. Based on a typical job description for this role, generate 10 likely behavioral interview questions I should prepare for."

- **Simulating a Mock Interview:** Prompt: "Let's do a mock interview. You are the hiring manager for a marketing internship. I am the student candidate. Ask me the first question. Wait for my response, and then provide constructive feedback on my answer and ask the next question."

⚙ ACTIVITY: YOUR AI CO-PILOT TEST FLIGHT

STEP 1: PICK A TASK:

Choose one simple task, like writing a single resume bullet point for your part-time job.

STEP 2: WRITE IT YOURSELF FIRST:

Write the best version you can on your own, using the A+Q formula in Chapter 11.

STEP 3: USE THE AI CO-PILOT:

Now, use one of the prompts above to ask AI for its version. Give it the same context.

STEP 4: COMPARE AND COMBINE:

Look at both versions. What did the AI do well? (Maybe it used a stronger action verb). What did it miss? (It didn't know the specific number of customers you helped). Now, create a final, 'hybrid' version that combines the AI's professional language with your authentic details. This is the co-pilot method in action.

THE BOTTOM LINE

AI is a tool, not a replacement for your own thought and effort. Use it to break through writer's block and make your own ideas sound more professional. The students who use AI as a strategic co-pilot will save time and produce better work. The ones who use it as an autopilot will sound generic and get lost in the crowd. Be the co-pilot.

I have been training an AI Coach with all of my writing, Intellectual Property, and personality. If you want advice based on my Talent Acquisition experience, visit Coach Julia AI at Hi2Hired.com.

FINDING YOUR SCENE: CHOOSING THE RIGHT EMPLOYER & INDUSTRY

Groundwork done. Map from Chapter 2 in hand. Internship types understood. Your true priorities? Pinpointed. Now, the real fun begins.

Now, it's time to put on your detective hat, but we're not looking for a specific job just yet. Before you can figure out what you want to do, you need to figure out where you want to do it.

Think of it like choosing a college. You didn't just apply to every school in the country. You thought about what kind of environment you wanted: Big university or small liberal arts college? A bustling city or a quiet college town? The 'best' school isn't the best for everyone. The same is true for companies. Finding the right type of employer is the first step in finding an internship you'll actually love.

THE GREAT DEBATE: BIG COMPANY VS. SCRAPPY STARTUP

One of your biggest choices? Company size. A massive corporation offers a wildly different experience than a five-person startup. Neither is inherently 'better'; they're just different.

The Blockbuster Movie (Big Corporations) These are the household names: Google, Apple, Amazon, AutoZone, or WalMart. Working here is like being on the set of a massive blockbuster film.

- **The Perks:**

    o **Structure & Resources:** They have huge budgets, established training programs, and a clear path for interns.

    o **Brand Name Recognition:** Having a big name on your resume is a powerful signal to future employers.

    o **A Big Intern Class:** You'll likely be part of a large group of interns, which means instant community, social events, and a great network.

- **The Reality:**

    o **You're a Specialist:** Your role might be very specific and narrow. You'll become an expert on one very small piece of the puzzle, and you might not see the whole picture.

    o **Things can Move Slowly:** Big companies can be bureaucratic. Getting an idea approved can take a lot of time and meetings.

    o **It's Harder to Stand Out:** In a sea of hundreds of interns, making a huge, individual impact can be more challenging.

    o **Limited Access to Leaders:** These companies have many layers and your visibility to Executive level leaders will be limited.

The Indie Film (Startups) These are the small, agile, and often chaotic companies trying to change the world from a garage or a co-working space. Working here is like being on the set of a passion project indie film.

- **The Perks:**

    o **You'll Wear Many Hats:** One day you're doing marketing, the next you're helping with product design, and the day after you're assembling office furniture. The learning curve is steep and exciting.

    o **High Impact:** The work you do can have a direct and immediate impact on the company's success.

    o **Direct Access to Leaders:** You might be working directly with the CEO or the founders.

- **The Reality:**

    o **Organized Chaos:** There might not be a formal training program or a clear structure. You have to be a self-starter who is comfortable with ambiguity.

    o **Fewer Resources:** Forget fancy perks. The budget is tight, and your internship might even be unpaid.

    o **Less Brand Recognition:** You'll have to explain what the company does to future employers (and maybe even your parents).

The Acclaimed TV Series (Mid-Sized Companies) These are the established but not-yet-famous companies. They often offer the best of both worlds: more structure than a startup, but more flexibility and impact than a massive corporation. Don't overlook these gems.

- **The Perks:**

  o **The 'Goldilocks' Zone:** You often get the best of both worlds, more structure and resources than a startup, but more flexibility and direct impact than a huge corporation.

  o **Real, Meaningful Work:** You're less likely to be a tiny cog in a giant machine. Interns are often given ownership of significant projects that directly contribute to the team's goals.

  o **More Visibility:** With fewer layers of management, you'll have more opportunities to interact with senior leaders and have your work noticed.

  o **Industry Recognition:** While not a household name, these companies are often highly respected leaders within their specific industry, which is a strong signal on your resume.

- **The Reality:**

  o **Fewer Bells and Whistles:** They may not have the flashy perks, massive intern parties, or global brand recognition of a tech giant.

  o **Growing Pains:** Processes might be less defined than at a large corporation but more rigid than at a startup as the company scales.

o **Smaller Intern Class:** The intern community will be smaller and potentially less structured than at a big company.

BEYOND SIZE: HOW TO FIND A COMPANY'S TRUE VIBE

Once you have a sense of the size you prefer, you need to investigate a company's culture. 'Culture' is just another word for a company's personality. Is it collaborative or competitive? Fast-paced or steady? Here's how you find out what a company is really like:

- **Read the Mission Statement (but be skeptical):** A company's 'About Us' page is what they want you to think they are. It's a good starting point, but it's just the movie trailer.

- **Scour Employee Reviews on Glassdoor:** This is the real, unfiltered audience review. Don't get hung up on one angry ex-employee, but look for patterns. Do dozens of reviews mention 'great work-life balance'? Or do they all complain about 'terrible management'? What jobs or locations are those people in? That's your clue.

- **Who Shows Up:** Identify employers by observing which companies sponsor or attend student-led organizations you support, such as NSBE (National Society of Black Engineers), SWE (Society of Women Engineers), O4U (Out for Undergrad), and others.

- **Stalk Social Media:** Check out the company's LinkedIn and Instagram. What do they post about? Do they celebrate their employees? Do they seem serious and corporate, or fun and creative? This is how the company presents their personality to the world.

Check the News: Do a quick Google News search for the company. Are they in the news for launching an innovative new product, or for a massive layoff?

💡 INSIDER INSIGHT: BEYOND THE FAMOUS LOGOS (B2B VS. B2C)

Most students only think about companies whose products they use every day, such as Nike, Apple, or Coca-Cola (these are called Business-to-Consumer, or B2C, companies). But you're missing a massive part of the economy: Business-to-Business (B2B) companies. These are the 'hidden champions' that sell products and services to other companies. Think about it: everyone knows Tesla (B2C), but who makes the specialized microchips that go into their cars? That B2B company is likely a global leader in its field and an incredible place for an engineering intern. Everyone knows about Spotify (B2C), but who provides the massive cloud infrastructure that allows them to stream music to millions? That B2B company is a tech giant. These companies often have amazing, less-competitive internship programs with more hands-on work. I have worked for several of these B2B companies in my career. We were always challenged in helping students understand what we do and the value of working for us instead of a 'brand' name. There are so many of these companies out there, I highly encourage you to walk up to their booth and talk to their representative at the next Career Fair. You may be surprised at how many cool non-brand name organizations there are out there and the amazing opportunities they provide.

⚙ ACTIVITY: BUILDING YOUR TARGET COMPANY HIT LIST

This activity will help you move from a vague idea to a concrete list of potential employers that are a great fit for you. Remember to think back to earlier chapters on identifying the type of internship experience you are looking for.

STEP 1: DEFINE YOUR VIBE

Check the box that best describes your ideal work environment.

- ☐ **Big Company:** Structure, resources, a big intern class.

- ☐ **Startup:** High impact, wearing many hats, fast-paced.

- ☐ **Mid-Sized:** A balance of both.

- ☐ **Fast-Paced & Changing:** I like when every day is different.

- ☐ **Stable & Predictable:** I like knowing what to expect.

- ☐ **Collaborative & Team-Oriented:** I do my best work with others.

- ☐ **Independent & Autonomous:** I like to own my work from start to finish.

STEP 2: BRAINSTORM YOUR INDUSTRIES

Based on your 'vibe' and your general interests, list three to five industries that seem like a good fit. Don't just think about what you're majoring in. Think about what you're passionate about.

- Examples: Renewable Energy, Video Game Development, Sustainable Fashion, Healthcare Technology, or Digital Media.

_____

STEP 3: CREATE YOUR HIT LIST

Now, pick one industry from your list above. Your mission is to find five specific companies in that industry that match your 'vibe.' Use LinkedIn, Google News, and industry-specific websites (like TechCrunch for tech or Adweek for advertising).

- Your Chosen Industry: _____

- Your 5 Target Companies:

  o A big, well-known leader _____

  o A fast-growing startup _____

  o A mid-sized company _____

  o A 'hidden champion' B2B _____

  o Your choice _____

STEP 4: EXPAND YOUR TARGET LIST:

Take your top five list of employers and feed it into AI with the following prompt. "Here are my top five target companies for a summer internship. Show me 25 additional companies that might offer similar intern experiences." You can refine this prompt to focus on a specific location, industry, or job title.

💡 INSIDER INSIGHT: THE COST OF A CULTURE MISMATCH

During a tough recession, a friend of mine eagerly accepted a job offer, prioritizing any paycheck over the right fit. She skipped a deep dive into the company's culture and values, which turned out to be the polar opposite of what she needed for growth and autonomy. Though grateful for the income, she was miserable within months, realizing the job was unsustainable without alignment to her core values. This harsh lesson solidified that understanding a company's culture and ensuring it aligns with your values isn't a luxury; it's non-negotiable for long-term career satisfaction. Always do your due diligence.

THE BOTTOM LINE

You now have a real, actionable 'hit list' of companies. You've moved from a vague idea of 'I need an internship' to a focused understanding of the types of places where you'd thrive. This isn't just a list; it's the foundation of a targeted, strategic search.

Now that you know the 'where,' we can finally start investigating the 'what.' In the next chapter, we'll take this target list and do a deep dive into the specific roles you might play at these companies.

PLAYING CAREER DETECTIVE: THE ROLE DEEP DIVE

Reconnaissance complete. Your target company 'hit list' from the last chapter is ready. You now know where you'd thrive.

Now, it's time to get granular and investigate the 'what.'

This chapter is where you put on your detective hat again, but this time you're not just looking at the company, you're investigating a specific role. We're going to take your target list and do a 'deep dive' to see what a career in a specific function at one of those companies really looks like. My goal is to help you get a sneak peek behind the curtain of the professional world.

WHY WE'RE PLAYING DETECTIVE (AGAIN)

This deep dive is more than just research; it's about building a clear, realistic picture of your potential future. A job title on a website tells you almost nothing about the reality of the work. This investigation is your way of preventing the classic 'dream job' disappointment. By the end of this chapter, you will:

- **Know the Day-to-Day Reality:** The title 'Marketing Associate' means little without understanding the daily reality. Will you be analyzing spreadsheets or storyboarding video campaigns? Knowing the routine is the only way to confirm if the work truly fits you.

- **See if the Work Is Actually Interesting:** Every job is about solving problems. The question is, which problems do you find exciting? Discovering the core challenges of a role helps you figure out if you'll be energized by the work or just counting down the hours until Friday.

- **Create a Personal Learning Roadmap:** This is where you start building the resume for the job you want, not just the one you have. By identifying the exact skills that are in high demand, you can see where you're already strong and create a smart, targeted plan to learn the rest.

- **Map Out Your Future:** This process helps you see the difference between a job and a career. You'll start to see how people grow, what the next steps look like, and how an entry-level job can lead to incredible opportunities five or 10 years down the line.

💡 INSIDER INSIGHT: THE DETECTIVE CANDIDATE

When I reviewed applications, I could immediately spot the 'detectives.' Their cover letters and resumes didn't just say, "I'm a hard worker who is passionate about marketing." They said something specific, such as, "I was excited to see your company is expanding into podcast advertising, as I've been studying audio editing on my own and believe my skills could contribute to that initiative." The better applicant didn't just want an internship; they understood what our company was doing and connected their skills to our specific needs. That's the person whose application immediately went to the top of the pile. This deep dive is how you find those details that make you stand out.

⚙️ACTIVITY: YOUR FIRST CASE FILE, THE ROLE DEEP DIVE

It's time to open your first case file. In the last chapter, you created your 'Internship Focus Statement.' That statement is your starting hypothesis. Now, like any good detective, you're going to gather evidence to see if your hypothesis holds up in the real world.

STEP 1: STATE YOUR HYPOTHESIS

Based on your Focus Statement, write down what you believe will be a good fit for you.

- **Example:** "I believe a role in digital marketing at a mission-driven company will be a good fit for my values and creative skills."

My Hypothesis: _____

_____

_____

STEP 2: PICK YOUR TARGET ROLE

Look at your 'Hit List' of companies from Chapter 7. Choose ONE company and a potential role within it to investigate first.

My Target for Investigation: (e.g., 'Software Engineer Intern at Google,' or 'Brand Management Intern at Procter & Gamble')

STEP 3: GATHER YOUR INTEL

Now, use the internet to gather evidence about your target role. Your goal is to get a 360-degree view.

- **The Mission Brief (Job Descriptions):** Search LinkedIn, Indeed, or the company's career site for two to three real internship or entry-level job descriptions for your target role. What specific tasks and projects keep showing up? What tools or software do they mention?

- **The "A Day in the Life" Recon:** This is a detective's secret weapon. Go to YouTube and search for "A Day in the Life of a [job title] at [Company Name]." Watch a few videos. Does the daily routine look exciting or draining?

- **The Career Path Map:** On LinkedIn, look at the profiles of people who currently have your target role at that company. Where did they work before? What was their major? Where do people in this role go next? This shows you the potential career journey.

STEP 4: THE SKILL SHOWDOWN (YOUR PERSONAL GAP ANALYSIS)

Look at the job descriptions you found. List the top five to seven skills they require. Now, honestly assess where you stand with each one. This isn't about judging yourself; it's about creating a smart action plan.

P = Possess. I'm confident in this skill. F = Foundational. I have some basic knowledge or experience. L = Learning. This is a skill I need to build.

Required Skill from Job Description | My Status (P/F/L) *Example: Python Programming L*

STEP 5: MY ACTION PLAN

Now, pick one to two skills you marked as (L) or (F). What is one concrete step you can take this month to start building that skill?

- **Example:** "For Python (L), I will sign up for a free 'Intro to Python' course on Coursera and complete the first two modules."

  Skill to Build: _____

  Action Step: _____

  Action Step: _____

  Skill to Build: _____

  Action Step: _____

  Action Step: _____

STEP 6: THE FINAL VERDICT

You've gathered the evidence. Now it's time to close the case file. Based on everything you've learned, answer these questions:

- Was your hypothesis correct? Does this role and industry seem like a good fit for you? Why or why not?

- What was the most surprising thing you learned during your investigation?

- What is your next move? (e.g., "I'm even more excited now and will start tailoring my resume," or "This wasn't what I expected, so I'm going to open a new case file on my second-choice career path.")

WHAT IF YOU'RE STILL STUCK?

Sometimes, even a good detective hits a dead end. You might do all this research and still feel unsure. That is completely normal. It doesn't mean you failed; it just means you need more information. If you're feeling stuck, it's often a sign that you need to move from online research to human research. The next step is to talk to people who are actually doing the job. We'll cover exactly how to do that with informational interviews later in the book, but for now, just know that feeling uncertain is part of the process.

THE BOTTOM LINE

You just did something most students never do. You went beyond the job title and investigated the reality of a career path. You've moved from a vague idea to a clear, evidence-based understanding of where you might fit in the professional world.

Whether your investigation confirmed your hypothesis or sent you in a new direction, you are now making decisions based on data, not just daydreams or hearsay. You have a clear sense of your strengths and a real action plan to fill any gaps.

WINNING THE MENTAL GAME: NAVIGATING IMPOSTER SYNDROME, COMPARISON, AND BURNOUT

We've covered strategy, maps, targets, and tools. Now, let's get real: the toughest part of the internship search often isn't the resume or the interview. It's the grueling mental game.

It's the gut-punch feeling you get when you see a friend post their 'dream internship' announcement on LinkedIn, and you're still searching. It's the quiet voice in your head that whispers, 'Am I really qualified for this?' during the interview process. And it's the sheer exhaustion of trying to stay motivated when you're juggling applications, classes, and a social life.

This chapter is about tackling those challenges head-on. Because the most brilliant strategy in the world won't work if you're too burnt out or discouraged to execute it.

THE SOCIAL MEDIA COMPARISON TRAP

You scroll. There it is: a classmate, beaming in front of a fancy office, caption starting, 'I'm so excited to announce ... ' Instantly, your stomach drops. The spiral begins: 'They got that internship? I applied there and heard nothing. What am I doing wrong? Am I falling behind?'

This is the Social Media Comparison Trap, and it is brutal. It turns a platform (LinkedIn) for professional connection into a highlight reel of everyone else's success, making you feel like you're the only one struggling.

Why it happens: Social media is curated. People are sharing their polished successes, not the countless rejections or the hard work behind the scenes. Your brain, however, tends to compare your messy, real-time journey to their seemingly perfect outcomes. It's easy to forget that you're only seeing a fraction of their story, and you're comparing your 'behind the scenes' to their 'highlight reel.'

Let's reframe this. LinkedIn is not reality. It's a performance. People only post their wins, never their rejections, their self-doubt, or the 50 applications they sent that went into a black hole.

THE STRATEGY: PUT ON YOUR BLINDERS

- **Curate Your Feed:** Mute or unfollow accounts that trigger your anxiety. Follow companies, industry leaders, and content that inspires and educates you, not content that makes you feel small.

- **Log Off:** Set a timer for your LinkedIn sessions. Get in, do your research or networking, and get out. Don't fall into the endless scroll.

- **Remember Your Own Timeline:** Your career path is yours alone. The student who gets a prestigious internship as a sophomore might burn out by the time they're 25. The student who struggles and has to hustle for their first role often builds a resilience that serves them for their entire career. Run your own race.

BEATING IMPOSTER SYNDROME: THAT 'AM I GOOD ENOUGH?' FEELING

Imposter syndrome: that nagging voice whispering you're a fraud, that any moment, someone will 'find you out.' You see a job asking for five skills; you have four. Yet, you fixate on the missing one, thinking, 'I can't apply.'

- **Why it happens:** As a student, you're in a constant state of learning, which means you're always aware of what you don't know. The professional world, however, values what you can do and your potential to learn the rest.

THE STRATEGY: GATHER YOUR EVIDENCE

- **Go Back to Your 'Experience Inventory':** Look at the list of experiences you made in Chapter 1. Look at the skills you've learned. You have tangible proof of your abilities.

- **Focus on 'Foundational' Skills:** Remember the 'P/F/L' (Possess / Foundational / Learning) scale from your detective work? Recruiters don't expect interns to be experts. They are hiring for potential. Having a 'Foundational' level in a skill is often more than enough.

- **Reframe the Job Description:** A job description is a wish list, not a checklist. I've written hundreds of them. We often put everything we could possibly want in a candidate, knowing that no single person will have it all. If you meet 60% - 70% of the qualifications, you are a strong candidate.

💡 INSIDER INSIGHT: WE HIRE FOR POTENTIAL, NOT PERFECTION

I can't tell you how many times I've hired an intern who didn't have every single 'required' skill on the job description. I once hired a student for a data-heavy role who had never used the specific software we listed. Why? Because in her interview, she told a brilliant story about a class project where she had to learn a different, complex software tool in two weeks to get the job done. That story told me more than a keyword on a resume ever could. It told me she was a fast learner, resourceful, and not afraid of a challenge. We can teach you software; we can't teach you that kind of drive.

STAYING MOTIVATED: HOW TO RUN THE MARATHON

The internship search is a marathon, not a sprint. There will be days and weeks where you feel like you're making no progress. Burnout is real, and it can derail your entire search.

THE STRATEGY: SMALL WINS AND SMART BREAKS

- **Set Micro-Goals:** Instead of a huge, daunting goal like 'Get an internship,' set small, achievable goals for each week. "This week, I will tailor my resume for two jobs, find three alumni to connect with on LinkedIn, and watch one 'Day in the Life' video." Checking these off provides a sense of progress and momentum.

- **Schedule 'No-Search' Time:** You cannot and should not be job searching 24/7. Schedule time in your week where you are not allowed to think about it. Go for a run, watch a movie, or hang out with friends. Your brain needs rest to perform at its best.

- **Celebrate the Process, not Just the Outcome:** Did you send out five tailored applications this week? That's a win. Did you have a great informational interview, even if it didn't lead to a job? That's a win. Acknowledge and celebrate these small victories. They are the fuel that will get you through the marathon.

⚙ ACTIVITY: YOUR MENTAL GAME PLAN

This activity is about creating a personalized toolkit to help you stay confident and motivated.

STEP 1: YOUR COMPARISON CURE:

- Write down the name of one person or type of post on social media that makes you feel anxious or behind. Now, make a commitment to mute, unfollow, or hide that content.

- List three inspiring industry leaders, companies, or creators you will follow instead to make your feed a source of motivation, not stress.

STEP 2: YOUR IMPOSTER SYNDROME 'PROOF FILE':

- Look back at all the work you've done in this book. List three concrete accomplishments, a project you're proud of, a skill you've developed, or a part-time job where you made an impact, that you can look at when you start to feel like you're not qualified. This is your personal evidence file.

STEP 3: YOUR ANTI-BURNOUT PLAN:

- What is one non-negotiable 'no-search' activity you will schedule for yourself this week? (e.g., "Friday night, I will not open my laptop.")

- What is a small, process-oriented goal you will set for yourself this week? (e.g., "I will draft one personalized cover letter.")

THE BOTTOM LINE

The internship search is as much an emotional journey as it is a professional one. It's normal to feel overwhelmed, but it's not okay to let that feeling derail you. By actively managing your mindset, you're not just improving your chances of landing an internship; you're building the resilience and confidence that will define your entire career.

If you try some of the approaches listed in this chapter and you are still feeling down or depressed, visit your campus career center or talk to a supportive friend.

Now that you've shored up your mental game, let's start building the tools that will tell your powerful story.

PART II:
GETTING YOUR STORY STRAIGHT:
RESUMES, LINKEDIN, AND
HOW TO NOT SOUND BORING

Your application materials are your marketing ads. Here's how to make them compelling, not just a list of stuff you've done.

WHAT'S YOUR STORY?: HOW TO NOT SOUND LIKE EVERY OTHER STUDENT IN THE WORLD

Let's be honest: 'personal brand' probably makes you cringe. I get it. It sounds like something for reality TV stars or Instagram influencers, not for a student just trying to land a decent internship.

But here's the secret: you already have a personal brand. You do. I swear.

Jeff Bezos, the Amazon guy, said, "Your personal brand is what people say about you when you aren't in the room." This is one of my all-time favorite quotes because it's brutally true. Your brand is your reputation. It's the vibe you give off. It's the story people tell themselves about you after they meet you for five minutes or scan your LinkedIn profile for 10 seconds.

The only question is, are you going to be the one to write that story, or are you going to let someone else write it for you?

WHY YOUR STORY IS YOUR SECRET WEAPON

In a sea of identical majors and similar GPAs, your personal brand is what makes you, well, you. When I was a recruiter, I'd look at a stack of resumes that all looked the same. Same classes, same part-time jobs, same everything. It was boring. Then, I'd find a profile that told a story. That person immediately went to the top of the pile.

Here's why this matters more than ever:

- **You Control the Narrative.** If you don't define yourself, a recruiter will do it for you. And they'll do it in about five seconds. They'll see 'Finance Major' and think, 'Okay, another finance major.' But if you define yourself as a "Finance student passionate about using data to find market trends," suddenly you're not just another student. You're a specialist in the making.

- **You Stand out From the Crowd.** Your brand is your unique mix of skills, experiences, passions, and quirks. Maybe you're a history major who is obsessed with video game design. That's not weird; that's a brand! It tells me you understand narrative, research, and technology. You're interesting. You're memorable.

- **It Makes Networking Less Awkward.** When you know your story, the dreaded 'Tell me about yourself' question becomes easy. It's not a test. It's an invitation to share your brand. It gives you a script that feels natural because it's true.

- **It's an Opportunity Magnet.** A clear, consistent brand doesn't just help you find jobs; it helps jobs find you. Recruiters are searching LinkedIn every single day for keywords. When your profile tells a clear story, you start showing up in the right searches, sometimes for jobs that haven't even been posted yet.

💡INSIDER INSIGHT: THE TWO MARKETING STUDENTS

I'll never forget two students who applied for the same marketing internship. On paper, they were identical. Same school, same major, same 3.7 GPA. Student #1's LinkedIn headline said: "Student at the University of Tennessee." Her profile was basically a list of her classes. Yawn. Student #2's LinkedIn headline said: "Marketing Student Passionate about Community Building & Digital Storytelling." Her profile mentioned her volunteer work managing social media for a local animal shelter and had a link to a simple blog where she analyzed Super Bowl commercials. Who got the interview? It wasn't even a contest. Student #2 got the call. She wasn't just a student; she was a storyteller. She was a community builder. She made it easy for me to see exactly how she could help my team. She told me her story.

THE THREE PARTS OF YOUR STORY

Your brand isn't some big, complicated thing. It's really just these three pieces working together. Here's the blueprint.

- **Your Pitch (Your Story):** This is your 30-second answer to "What are you all about?" It connects what you've done in the past (even if it's just a class project or a part-time job) to what you want to do in the future.

- **Your Digital Handshake (Your Online Vibe):** This is your LinkedIn profile, first and foremost. It's your professional storefront. If it's incomplete or unprofessional, it's like showing up to an interview with a giant stain on your shirt. It's the first thing people will judge.

- **How You Show Up (Your Professionalism):** This is everything else. The way you write an email. The way you listen on a video call. The fact that you show up on time. It's the part of your brand that proves you're reliable, respectful, and someone people actually want to work with.

💡 INSIDER INSIGHT: THE ESCAPE ROOM EXPERT

I once coached a student who was convinced she had no brand. She was an accounting major with average grades and a part-time job at a pizza place. But as we talked, she lit up when she mentioned her obsession with escape rooms. She did them all the time. She even designed one for a sorority event. I said, "That's it. That's your brand." She looked at me like I was crazy. But think about it. What does an escape room expert do? They work with a diverse team under intense pressure. They find hidden clues and analyze complex information to solve problems against a deadline. That's not just a hobby; that's a perfect description of a great auditor or financial analyst. She added this to her LinkedIn 'About' section. In her next interview, the hiring manager spent ten minutes asking her about it. She got the internship. Why? Because she didn't sound like every other accounting student. She had a story.

⚙️ACTIVITY: FIND YOUR 3-WORD BRAND DNA

Before you can write your story, you need to know the main characters: your core strengths. This isn't a test. Don't overthink it.

STEP 1: YOUR THREE WORDS

Look over your skills, your values, and your interests. If you had to describe your professional self in just three words, what would they be? Write down the first three that come to mind.

- Examples:

    o Analytical, Curious, Problem-Solver

    o Creative, Strategic, Communicator

    o Organized, Dependable, Team-Player

    o Empathetic, Detailed, Researcher

Your Three Words: _____

_____   _____

STEP 2: BUILD YOUR DNA STATEMENT

Now, take those three words and combine them into a single sentence that starts with "I am ... " This is the foundation of your pitch.

- Example:

    o Words: Creative, Strategic, Communicator

    o Statement: "I am a creative problem solver who loves using strategic thinking to communicate big ideas in a simple way."

Your DNA Statement: I am_____

_____

_____

THE BOTTOM LINE

Your personal brand isn't about being fake or creating a 'persona.' It's the exact opposite. It's about digging deep, finding what is genuinely interesting and unique about you, and then making it easy for the rest of the world to see it. In a world where everyone is trying to fit in, your brand is what helps you stand out. Stop trying to be the perfect, cookie-cutter candidate you think they want. Start being more of who you actually are. That's the brand that gets the job.

YOUR RESUME IS A MARKETING AD, NOT A HISTORY REPORT

Staring at a blank resume page? Feels impossible, right? You're thinking, 'What have I even done?' It's easy to dismiss that barista gig or history project as 'not real experience.'

I'm here to tell you that's wrong. You have more experience than you think. The secret isn't having the 'perfect' background; it's learning how to tell the story of the background you do have in a way that gets a recruiter excited.

Research shows recruiters typically spend only six to eight seconds reviewing a resume before making a decision. Your resume doesn't just need to be ATS-friendly; it needs to be compelling and incredibly easy for a human to digest, fast. This chapter is your step-by-step guide to building that story.

THE MODERN RESUME: YOUR PERSONAL MARKETING AD

Think of your resume not as a history report, but as a 30-second commercial for your professional brand. Every word, every bullet point, should be designed to convince the viewer (the recruiter) of one thing: "This person can add value to my company." This isn't about just listing keywords; it's about making it immediately clear how your skills and experiences align with what the company needs.

THE A+Q FORMULA: YOUR STORYTELLING TOOLS

Every powerful resume is built on two simple but critical ingredients: **Action Verbs + Quantifiable Results.** This is the A+Q formula, and it's how you turn a boring list of tasks into a compelling story of impact.

ACTION VERBS: THE POWER OF DOING

Recruiters look for candidates who do things. Using strong action verbs at the beginning of your bullet points makes your accomplishments pop. They transform passive descriptions into dynamic showcases of your initiative.

- **Why it matters:** When I review resumes, my eyes go straight to those verbs. They tell me you're not passive; you take action and deliver results. A resume packed with powerful action verbs immediately signals, "This student doesn't just show up, they make things happen."

Here's a list of powerful action verbs, grouped to help you think about different ways to highlight your contributions.

- **Leadership / Management:** Led, Oversaw, Coordinated, Directed, Guided, Managed, Supervised, Mentored, Organized, Chaired

- **Communication / Collaboration:** Communicated, Collaborated, Presented, Liaised, Negotiated, Wrote, Edited, Articulated, Convinced, Facilitated

- **Analytical / Problem-Solving:** Analyzed, Researched, Evaluated, Diagnosed, Resolved, Assessed, Interpreted, Investigated, Optimized, Tested

- **Creative / Design:** Designed, Developed, Created, Illustrated, Conceptualized, Produced, Implemented, Formulated, Launched, Pitched

- **Technical / Programming:** Coded, Programmed, Developed, Built, Configured, Implemented, Debugged, Maintained, Deployed, Automated

- **Financial / Data:** Audited, Budgeted, Calculated, Forecasted, Generated, Processed, Reconciled, Reduced, Increased, Streamlined

- **Project Management:** Planned, Executed, Managed, Scheduled, Tracked, Delegated, Coordinated, Delivered, Achieved, Initiated

QUANTIFIABLE ACHIEVEMENTS: SHOW, DON'T JUST TELL

Here's the golden rule of resume writing: quantify your impact. Numbers offer clear, undeniable proof of your accomplishments. They give context and weight to your contributions, making them concrete and memorable.

- **Why it Matters to a Recruiter (and a Hiring Manager):** Quantified results speak a universal language: impact. Whenever I saw numbers on a resume, I knew that candidate understood outcomes, not just tasks. It shows they think like a contributor focused on delivering measurable value. That mindset stands out every time, because it helps me imagine the tangible impact you could have for my team.

HOW TO QUANTIFY ANYTHING (OR ALMOST ANYTHING):

- **Numbers:** How many? How much? How often? (e.g., "Processed 50 invoices," "Trained 10 new volunteers," "Served an average of 75 customers per shift")

- **Percentages:** By what percentage? (e.g., "Reduced errors by 15%," "Increased efficiency by 10%," "Improved customer satisfaction scores by 5%")

- **Time:** How quickly? How much time saved? (e.g., "Completed tasks two days ahead of schedule," "Reduced response time by 50%," "Streamlined a process, saving the team five hours per week")

- **Money:** How much saved or generated? (e.g., "Saved $500 in supply costs," "Generated $1,000 in sales," "Identified cost-saving measures totaling $200 for club events")

- **Scale:** How large was the project, team, or impact? (e.g., "Managed a $2,000 budget," "Supported a team of eight," "Impacted 100+ users," "Organized events for a student body of 500+")

- **Frequency:** How regularly did you perform a task or achieve a result? (e.g., "Published three articles weekly," "Facilitated weekly team meetings," "Processed payroll for 20 employees bi-weekly")

RESUME SECTIONS DEEP DIVE: BUILDING YOUR STORY, PIECE BY PIECE

Let's build your resume from the top down, making every section count. Each section is a puzzle piece contributing to the full picture of your potential.

- **Contact Information:** Keep it clean and professional. Include your full name, phone number, a professional-sounding email, and your LinkedIn profile URL. Make it easy for a potential employer to reach you.

- **Professional Summary or Objective:** This is the headline of your commercial. It's your chance to grab attention immediately and frame your entire resume.

    o **Objective (Best for first-time interns or career changers):** Focuses on your goals and what you aim to contribute. *Example: "Enthusiastic Business Administration student seeking a Marketing Internship to apply foundational knowledge in market research, content creation, and social media skills in a fast-paced corporate setting to drive brand engagement."*

    o **Summary (Best if you have some experience or clear career direction):** Highlights your top skills and relevant experiences upfront. *Example: "Highly motivated Computer Science student with a strong foundation in Python and Java. Proven ability to develop full-stack applications through hands-on project work and collaborative problem solving, seeking a challenging Software Engineering Internship to contribute to innovative software solutions."*

- **Education:** Include your university, degree, major(s), minor(s), and expected graduation date. Include GPA only if it's 3.0 or higher (or higher if the industry/role typically requires a specific GPA, like finance). Add a 'Relevant Coursework' subsection to showcase specific knowledge that directly aligns with the internship.

- **Experience:** This is where you tell your A+Q stories. For each role, include your title, organization, location, and dates. Use two to four compelling bullet points per role, starting each with a strong action verb and incorporating quantifiable results. Even seemingly unrelated jobs can show valuable transferable skills.

- **Projects:** Your secret weapon. This is where you prove you can apply what you've learned and take initiative. Give the project a clear title, describe the goal, your specific role, the skills / tools you used, and the quantifiable outcome or impact. This section speaks volumes about your drive and practical abilities.

- **Skills:** Make this section clean and easy to scan. Group skills into logical categories (e.g., Programming Languages, Software, Data Analysis Tools, Languages, Soft Skills). This helps both the ATS and the human reader quickly identify your competencies.

ADDRESSING THE 'I HAVE NO EXPERIENCE' PANIC

Recruiters for internship programs are not looking for a 10-year work history. We are looking for potential. Your job is to translate the experiences you do have into the language of professional skills. Every experience you've had, whether it's in a classroom, a club, or a part-time job, has equipped you with valuable abilities. The key is to recognize and articulate them.

- **Academic Projects are Experience:** Treat your big school projects like a job on your resume. These demonstrate your ability to apply theoretical knowledge, work in teams, and deliver results.

  o *Before:* "Completed a group project for my marketing class."

  o *After:* **Marketing Strategy Case Study** | Principles of Marketing Course

    ▪ Analyzed market data for a local coffee shop to identify a new target audience of university students.

    ▪ Developed a comprehensive digital marketing plan projected to increase foot traffic by 15%.

    ▪ Collaborated with a four-person team to create a final presentation, which earned a 95% grade.

- **Your Part-Time Job is Experience:** Your job as a barista, retail associate, or server has taught you valuable professional skills.

  o *Before:* "Barista - Took orders and made coffee."

  o *After:* **Barista** | Campus Coffee Shop

    ▪ Assisted 100+ customers daily in a fast-paced environment, maintaining a 98% order accuracy rate.

    ▪ Trained three new team members on point-of-sale systems and drink preparation standards.

    ▪ Resolved customer issues effectively, contributing to a 10% increase in positive online reviews over six months.

- **Club Leadership and Volunteer Work Counts as Experience:**

  o *Before:* "Member of the Programming Club."

  o *After:* **Event Coordinator** | University Programming Club

    - Organized a university-wide hackathon for over 200 participants, securing five corporate sponsorships.

    - Managed a $2,500 event budget, negotiating with vendors to reduce costs by 10%.

    - Led a team of 10 volunteers to coordinate event logistics, marketing, and day-of operations.

⚙️ ACTIVITY: TRANSFORM YOUR RESUME FROM HISTORY REPORT TO MARKETING AD

Goal: To help you identify your most compelling experiences and translate them into powerful, results-oriented bullet points that grab a recruiter's attention.

Instructions: Gather Your 'History Report': Find your current resume or make a list of all your past jobs, volunteer work, projects, and academic achievements. Think of this as the raw data, your personal history.

STEP 1: BECOME A 'VALUE DETECTIVE':

For each item on your list, ask yourself:

- What skills did I use or develop?

- What problems did I solve?

- What were the results or impact of my work? (Quantify whenever possible!)

- How does this experience relate to the kinds of internships I'm interested in?

STEP 2: IDENTIFY YOUR 'SELLING POINTS':

Based on your detective work, circle or highlight the experiences and results that you think would be most appealing to a potential employer in your target field. These are your key 'selling points.'

STEP 3: DRAFT YOUR 'MARKETING COPY':

Now, take those selling points and start writing new bullet points for your resume. Focus on starting with action verbs and clearly stating the result or impact of your work.

- **Instead of:** "Worked as a barista."

- **Try:** "Provided exceptional customer service in a high-volume cafe, consistently receiving positive feedback."

- **Instead of:** "Completed a history project."

- **Try:** "Researched and presented a comprehensive analysis of [historical event] for a university course, earning a [grade or specific feedback]."

STEP 4: TAILOR YOUR AD:

Remember that a good marketing ad is tailored to its audience. As you draft your bullet points, think about the specific internships you're applying for and adjust the language and focus to highlight the skills and experiences most relevant to those roles.

STEP 5: GET FEEDBACK ON YOUR 'AD':

Share your revamped resume bullet points with a trusted friend, family member, or career advisor. Ask them:

- Does this clearly communicate the value I can bring?

- Are the results and impacts easy to understand?

- Does it sound like a marketing ad or still like a history report?

💡INSIDER INSIGHT: SHOWCASING POTENTIAL

When a resume from a first- or second-year student comes across my desk, I'm not looking for a list of prior internships. I'm looking for clues that tell me about their potential. A well-described class project shows me they can apply theory to practice. A part-time job with quantified results shows me they are reliable and understand customer service. A leadership role in a club shows me they have initiative. Don't underestimate these experiences; they are exactly what we look for.

THE BOTTOM LINE

Your resume isn't just a list of what you've done; it's your personal marketing ad, designed to showcase the value you bring. By transforming your experiences from a history report into compelling, results-driven selling points, you'll grab the attention of recruiters and significantly increase your chances of landing that dream internship.

WHY THAT 'OPTIONAL' COVER LETTER IS YOUR SECRET WEAPON

You're on the application page, right? Next to the resume upload, you see it: 'Cover Letter (Optional).'

Your first thought is probably, 'YES! One less thing to do.' You drag, drop, submit, and move on. But in doing so, you've just walked away from one of your single biggest opportunities to stand out.

Think of it this way: your resume is the black-and-white box score of your career so far. It's the stats, the facts, the what-where-when. It's essential, but it's not the whole story. The cover letter is the color commentary. It's your chance to add personality, connect the dots for the recruiter, and explain why you are the perfect fit in a way that a list of bullet points never can.

When a job posting says 'optional,' what a recruiter is really saying is, "You don't have to do this, but we're going to pay close attention to the people who put in the extra effort."

WHY THIS 'OPTIONAL' LETTER IS YOUR SECRET WEAPON

As a recruiter, when I was on the fence about two equally qualified candidates, the cover letter was almost always the tiebreaker. Here's what a great cover letter tells me that a resume can't:

- **It shows you can write.** In almost any corporate job, clear written communication is a critical skill. Your cover letter is your first and best opportunity to provide a writing sample. A well-written letter is a huge green flag.

- **It proves you're genuinely interested.** A generic resume can be sent to 100 companies. A cover letter that mentions the company's specific projects or values tells me you're not just looking for *an* internship; you're interested in *this* internship.

- **It lets you tell a story.** Do you have a non-traditional major? Did a specific life experience lead you to this career path? The cover letter is where you can explain the 'why' behind the facts on your resume.

THE ANATOMY OF A COVER LETTER THAT ACTUALLY GETS READ

A great cover letter isn't a long, boring essay. It's a sharp, concise, and powerful three- or four-paragraph message designed to make a human connection.

The Hook (Your Opening Paragraph) Your first paragraph has one job: to grab the reader's attention and tell them why you're writing.

- **The Formula:** State the exact role you're applying for and where you saw it. Then, immediately connect your core passion or a key qualification to the company's mission or a specific project.

  o *Before (Boring):* "I am writing to apply for the Marketing Intern position I saw on LinkedIn."

  o *After (Compelling):* "I am writing to express my keen interest in the Marketing Intern opportunity at [Company Name], as advertised on Handshake. As a Business Administration student passionate about understanding consumer behavior, I was incredibly excited by your recent campaign for [mention a specific product], which beautifully aligns with my interest in sustainable marketing."

The Core (Your 'Proof' Paragraphs) This is the heart of your letter. Your goal is to connect two or three of your most relevant experiences directly to the needs mentioned in the job description.

- **The Formula:** Pick a key requirement from the job description. Then, tell a short A+Q (Action + Quantifiable Result) story from your experience that proves you have that skill.

  o *Example:*

    ▪ Job Description asks for: "Experience managing social media."

    ▪ Your Cover Letter says: "As the Social Media Coordinator for my university's Marketing Club, I successfully managed content across Instagram and LinkedIn for over 150 members. By analyzing engagement metrics to refine our strategy, I was able to increase our overall engagement by 25% and boost event attendance by 15% in a single semester. This experience in content creation and audience analysis would allow me to quickly contribute to your brand initiatives."

The Close (Your 'Why This Company' Paragraph) End by reiterating your enthusiasm and making it clear why you want to work for them specifically.

- **The Formula:** Reiterate your excitement. Mention a specific company value, project, or aspect of their culture that resonates with you. End with a clear call to action.

  o *Example:* "I believe my ability to translate insights into engaging content, coupled with my strong organizational skills, would allow me to quickly contribute to your team. I am excited by the prospect of gaining hands-on experience at a leading consumer goods company and learning from the best in the industry. Thank you for your time and consideration. I welcome the opportunity to discuss my qualifications further."

INSIDER INSIGHT: THE 'WHY THIS COMPANY?' TEST

As a recruiter, I could immediately tell if a cover letter was just generic boilerplate. The best ones didn't just list what the student had done; they told me why they cared about my company. I still remember a student who opened her letter by referencing a sustainability initiative we'd just launched, connecting it to her passion for environmental policy. It was clear she hadn't just swapped in our company name on a template; she'd done her research and understood our values. That level of authenticity always caught my attention.

ACTIVITY: DRAFT YOUR SECRET WEAPON

Let's put this into practice. Grab your target job description from the last chapter's activity.

STEP 1: DECONSTRUCT THE JOB DESCRIPTION:

Make a list of the top three to four skills or qualifications the company is looking for.

STEP 2: MAP YOUR STORIES:

Next to each skill, write down one A+Q bullet point from your 'master resume' that proves you have that skill.

STEP 3: FIND YOUR 'WHY':

Spend five minutes on the company's website or LinkedIn page. Find one specific project, value, or recent news story that genuinely interests you.

STEP 4: DRAFT YOUR LETTER:

Using the three-part structure above, write a draft of your cover letter. Start with the compelling hook, use your A+Q stories to prove your value in the middle, and end with your personalized "why this company" closing.

PORTFOLIO (FOR CREATIVE / TECHNICAL ROLES): WHEN AND HOW TO SHOWCASE YOUR WORK

For roles in design, software development, data science, marketing, or any field where a visual demonstration of your skills adds value, a portfolio is essential. It's the ultimate 'show, don't just tell' tool.

- **When to Use It:** If the job description requests one, or if your field naturally relies on showcasing visual or technical work (e.g., UI/UX design, graphic design, web development, content creation, photography, or video editing). Even for data analysis or research-focused roles, a well-curated project portfolio can set you apart.

- **How to Build It:**

  o **Choose an Online Platform:** Use platforms like GitHub (for coding), Behance or Dribbble (for design), or build a simple personal website to host your work.

  o **Curate Your Best Projects:** Quality over quantity. Select three to five of your strongest, most relevant pieces.

  o **Show the Process, Not Just the Final Product:** For each project, explain your role, the problem you tackled, your process, and the results. Include visuals like screenshots, links to live demos, or code repositories.

○ **Keep it Professional:** Make sure your portfolio looks polished—clean design, intuitive navigation, and no broken links or unfinished pieces.

THE BOTTOM LINE

Your resume and cover letter are your crucial marketing documents. They must be strategic, tailored, and tell a compelling story of your impact. Focus on smart keyword alignment to pass the ATS, then use powerful, quantified accomplishments to grab the human recruiter's attention. A great resume doesn't just list what you've done; it proves what you can do.

This 'optional' cover letter field? It's a critical test of your initiative, communication, and genuine interest. While others take shortcuts, you have the chance to tell a story that makes a recruiter say, "I need to talk to this person."

Don't just submit a resume. Submit a story. That's your secret weapon.

YOUR 'USELESS' MAJOR IS A SUPERPOWER

History, English, philosophy, sociology, psychology—if that's your major (like mine was), you've heard it. Maybe from a well-meaning relative, a business school friend, or that quiet voice in your own head.

"What are you going to do with *that* major?"

It's a question that can make you feel like you're already behind in the internship race. Job descriptions demand Python, financial modeling, and SEO, and your heart sinks. You're smart, you work hard, but how do you connect a 20-page thesis on Renaissance art to an internship at a Fortune 500 company?

I get it. More than you know. As I mentioned in my intro, I was a psychology major at a university famous for its engineering and business programs. I was surrounded by students who had a clear, linear path from their classes to their co-op jobs. I felt like I was speaking a different language. I had to learn, on my own, how to translate my understanding of human behavior and research methods into the language of business.

This chapter is the translation guide I wish I'd had. Your major is not a liability. It has given you a set of powerful, in-demand skills that many business and engineering students lack. Your challenge isn't a lack of skills; it's a language barrier. Let's break it down.

THE CORPORATE ROSETTA STONE: TRANSLATING YOUR SKILLS

Companies might use business jargon, but what they're really looking for are people who can think, communicate, and solve complex problems. Your liberal arts education has trained you to be an expert in exactly that.

Here's your translation guide:

- If your skill is **Deep Research & Synthesis** (from writing a history thesis)... the business translation is **Market Analysis & Competitive Intelligence**.

- If your skill is **Deconstructing Arguments & Logic** (from a philosophy class)... the business translation is **Strategic Planning & Critical Thinking**.

- If your skill is **Crafting a Compelling Narrative** (from an English paper)... the business translation is **Content Strategy & Brand Storytelling**.

- If your skill is **Understanding Human Motivation & Behavior** (from a psychology course)... the business translation is **User Experience (UX) Research & Consumer Insights**.

- If your skill is **Analyzing Cultural Trends & Systems** (from a sociology class)... the business translation is **Diversity & Inclusion Strategy & Global Market Analysis**.

See the pattern? You have the skills. You just need to frame them in the context of business problems.

PUTTING IT ON PAPER: 'BEFORE AND AFTER' RESUME TRANSFORMATIONS

- **For the History Major (Targeting a Consulting Internship):**

  o *Before:* "Wrote a 30-page senior thesis on trade routes in the 15th-century Ottoman Empire."

  o *After:*

    - Conducted in-depth primary and secondary source research to analyze complex economic systems for a semester-long thesis project.

    - Synthesized qualitative data from over 50 historical documents to identify key economic trends and patterns.

    - Presented findings in a 30-page report, developing a clear narrative and defending my conclusions, which earned an A grade.

- **For the English Major (Targeting a Marketing Internship):**

  o *Before:* "Wrote essays analyzing Shakespearean literature."

  o *After:*

    - Analyzed complex narratives to deconstruct themes, character motivations, and audience reception in classic literature.

- Developed persuasive written arguments, crafting compelling stories to support a central thesis for 10+ analytical essays.

- Mastered editing and proofreading techniques to produce clear, concise, and error-free work under tight deadlines.

- For the Psychology Major (Targeting a User Experience (UX) Research Internship):

  o Before: "Studied human behavior and cognitive processes in psychology classes."

  o After:

    - Applied qualitative and quantitative research methods to analyze user interactions and inform product design in a capstone project.

    - Conducted user interviews and usability tests with 20+ participants to identify pain points and optimize user flows for a mobile application concept.

    - Translated complex psychological theories into actionable insights, presenting recommendations that improved user satisfaction by an estimated 10%.

- For the Sociology Major (Targeting a Diversity & Inclusion Internship):

  o Before: "Analyzed social structures and inequality for academic papers."

o After:

- Conducted sociological research to examine the impact of cultural systems on workplace dynamics and inclusivity for a semester-long study.

- Analyzed demographic data and qualitative feedback from 30+ individuals to identify patterns of engagement and belonging within community organizations.

- Developed a comprehensive presentation outlining key strategies for fostering equitable environments, presented to a panel of university faculty.

⚙ ACTIVITY: YOUR SUPERPOWER TRANSLATION

It's your turn. This activity will help you translate your unique academic experience into the language of business.

STEP 1: IDENTIFY YOUR CORE 'SUPERPOWER' SKILL

Think about your major. What is the single most important skill it has taught you? Is it research? Writing? Critical thinking? Empathy?

My Major's Superpower Skill is: _____

_____

STEP 2: FIND A TANGIBLE EXAMPLE

Think of one specific, significant project you completed for that major (a thesis, a major paper, a presentation, a research project).

My Example Project: _____

_____

STEP 3: THE 'BEFORE AND AFTER' TRANSFORMATION

Now, let's put it all together. Write a simple 'before' bullet point describing that project. Then, using the 'Corporate Rosetta Stone' and the examples above, write two to three powerful "after" bullet points that describe the same project in the language of business.

- **Before:** _____
- **After:** _____

💡 INSIDER INSIGHT: THE STORY IS EVERYTHING

I once interviewed a Sociology major for a role on our Diversity & Inclusion team. On paper, she had no direct HR experience. But in the interview, she told me about her senior project analyzing the social factors that impacted community engagement in different city neighborhoods. She talked about conducting interviews, analyzing survey data, and presenting her findings to a panel. She translated her academic project into a perfect case study for the exact skills we needed: research, empathy, and data analysis. She understood that we weren't hiring a sociologist; we were hiring someone who could understand people. She got the internship, and she was phenomenal.

THE BOTTOM LINE

Your major is not your limitation; it's your unique advantage. While other students were learning the 'what' in their business classes, you were mastering the 'how' and the 'why.' You learned how to think, how to reason, and how to communicate. In a world where technology is changing so fast that specific technical skills can become obsolete in a few years, these foundational human skills are more valuable than ever. Your job isn't to apologize for your major. It's to own it.

YOUR DIGITAL STOREFRONT: BUILDING A KILLER LINKEDIN PROFILE

Resume honed? Great. Now, build your digital headquarters. In today's recruiting landscape, your LinkedIn profile isn't just a digital resume; it's your professional storefront. A passive, resume-like profile is the bare minimum. A strategic, 'All-Star' profile is what gets you noticed.

A vast majority of recruiters use a powerful tool called LinkedIn Recruiter to actively hunt for candidates. When I get a new job opening, my first move isn't to post it; it's to start looking on LinkedIn. Your job is to make your profile a magnet for that search.

THE ALL-STAR PROFILE: WHY IT MATTERS

LinkedIn gives 'All-Star' status to fully completed profiles, and they've confirmed that these profiles get significantly more views. More profile views mean more opportunities for the candidate.

THE FIRST IMPRESSION (THE 3-SECOND TEST)

- **Your Professional Photo:** This is non-negotiable. Profiles with a professional photo get up to 14 times more views.

  o *The Rule:* A high-resolution, front-facing headshot of you, and only you, smiling genuinely.

  o *Example:* A clear, friendly headshot where you are dressed in business casual attire, looking directly at the camera. Avoid selfies, group photos, or heavily filtered images. Think approachable and professional, not a glamorous selfie or a blurry group shot from last weekend.

- **The Background Banner:** Your personal billboard.

  o *The Mistake:* Leaving the default blue constellation banner. This is a massive wasted opportunity. It's like leaving a giant, blank billboard in Times Square.

  o *The Strategy:* Your banner should visually communicate your passion or profession. Use a free tool like Canva to create a banner that reflects your aspirations.

  o *Examples:*

    - **For a Computer Science Student:** A stylized image of code, a circuit board, or a futuristic city skyline. Think abstract, clean, and subtly tech-oriented.

    - **For a Marketing Student:** A collage of social media icons, a graphic design pattern, or an abstract image representing creativity and communication. Maybe a subtle gradient or a mosaic of marketing-related symbols.

- **For a Business Student:** A professional-looking graphic with subtle financial charts, a cityscape, or a minimalist design reflecting professionalism and growth. Keep it sophisticated and understated.

YOUR HEADLINE: THE MOST IMPORTANT REAL ESTATE ON LINKEDIN

Your headline is the single most heavily weighted section for keyword searches. This isn't just a job title; it's your personal search engine optimization.

- **The Formula:** Aspiring [Target Role] | [Your Major] Student | [Two to Three Key Skills / Keywords]

- **Winning Examples:**

  o Aspiring Software Engineer | Computer Science Student | Python, Java, Cloud Computing

  o Aspiring Brand Management Intern | Marketing & Communications Student | Social Media Strategy, Content Creation, Market Research

  o **For a Finance Major:** Aspiring Financial Analyst | Business Administration Student | Data Analysis, Financial Modeling, Investment Research

  o **For a Communications Major:** Aspiring Public Relations Specialist | Communications Student | Media Relations, Crisis Management, Strategic Messaging

- **For a Premed Student:** Aspiring Medical Professional | Biology Student | Scientific Research, Patient Care, Healthcare Administration

- **For an Environmental Studies Major:** Aspiring Sustainability Consultant | Environmental Science Student | Data Analysis, Policy Research, Community Engagement

YOUR STORY: THE 'ABOUT' SECTION

This is your cover letter, elevator pitch, and personal story rolled into one. Write it in the first person ('I') and let your authentic self shine through. This is where you connect the dots for the recruiter.

- **Paragraph 1: The Present & The Future.** Start with a powerful opening sentence declaring your passion and career goals. Paint a picture of who you are and where you're headed.

  o *Example:* "I am a passionate Computer Science student at the University of Tennessee, driven by a desire to develop innovative software solutions that simplify complex challenges. My goal is to leverage my analytical skills and growing expertise in programming to contribute to impactful tech projects that genuinely make a difference."

- **Paragraph 2: The Past (Your Proof).** Connect your experiences to your goals using the A+Q formula. Show, don't just tell, how your past actions align with your future aspirations.

o *Example:* "During my coursework, I developed a Python-based application to automate data analysis for a research project, reducing processing time by 30% and improving data accuracy. I also actively participate in my university's Hackathon team, where I collaborated with peers to design and implement a mobile app concept that won the 'Most Innovative Solution' award, showcasing my ability to innovate under pressure."

- **Paragraph 3: The Call to Action & Keywords.** Reiterate your enthusiasm and add a 'Key Skills' line with your top keywords. Make it easy for recruiters to see your value and encourage them to connect.

o *Example:* "I am eager to apply my foundational knowledge and problem-solving abilities to a dynamic software engineering internship. I am particularly interested in roles where I can continue to build my skills in full-stack development and artificial intelligence within an innovative team. Key Skills: Python, Java, SQL, Agile Methodologies, Problem Solving, Team Collaboration, Data Analysis."

PROVING YOUR VALUE: THE EXPERIENCE & PROJECTS SECTIONS

These sections are your opportunity to demonstrate concrete achievements and skills. Every experience, no matter how small, can be framed to showcase your potential.

- **The Experience Section:** Every job is relevant. Frame it professionally with two to four quantified bullet points for each role, using the A+Q formula. Even a part-time job or volunteer role can highlight valuable transferable skills.

- *Example (Retail Associate - showing customer service, sales, teamwork):*

  - Provided exceptional customer service to 50+ customers daily in a fast-paced retail environment, consistently receiving positive feedback for product knowledge and issue resolution.

  - Managed cash register operations and processed transactions accurately, handling an average of $800 in daily sales while adhering to strict company policies.

  - Collaborated effectively with a team of 10 to maintain a clean and organized sales floor, contributing to a 15% increase in visual merchandise appeal during peak seasons.

- *Example (University Research Assistant - showing research, data handling, collaboration):*

  - Assisted lead researcher in collecting and organizing qualitative data from 30+ participant interviews for a study on social media engagement trends.

  - Utilized Excel to track and analyze survey responses, identifying key patterns that contributed to the final research report.

  - Collaborated with a team of three to present weekly progress updates, ensuring project milestones were met on schedule.

- **The Secret Weapon: The 'Projects' Section:** For students with limited formal internships or work experience, this is where you prove your skills. This section allows you to showcase hands-on learning and initiative.

o *Example (Personal Project - showcasing coding, problem-solving, real-world application):*

- **Personal Budget Tracker Application (Python & Flask)**

  - Designed and developed a full-stack web application using Python and Flask to empower users in tracking personal income and expenses.

  - Implemented user authentication and a PostgreSQL database to securely store financial data, ensuring data integrity and accessibility for 10+ test users.

  - Utilized Pandas for data analysis to generate weekly and monthly spending reports, providing users with actionable insights into their financial habits and fostering better financial literacy.

o *Example (Academic Project - showcasing analytical skills, presentation, teamwork):*

- **Sustainable Urban Development Plan (Urban Planning Course)**

  - Conducted in-depth research on urban infrastructure and environmental policies for a proposed sustainable neighborhood development project.

- Developed a comprehensive economic model forecasting resource consumption and potential cost savings, projecting a 20% reduction in utility expenses.

- Collaborated with a five-person interdisciplinary team to create a 45-minute presentation for city council members, outlining actionable recommendations and receiving an 'Outstanding Project' commendation.

THE 'TRUST SIGNALS': SKILLS & RECOMMENDATIONS

- **Skills & Endorsements:** This is pure keyword optimization. Members who list at least five skills receive up to 17 times more profile views.

  - *Strategy:* List at least 10-15 relevant skills. Ask classmates, professors, and mentors to endorse your skills.

  - *Examples of Skills Categories:*

    - **Software Development:** Python, Java, C++, JavaScript, SQL, Git, AWS, Full-Stack Development

    - **Marketing:** Social Media Marketing, Content Creation, SEO, Google Analytics, Market Research, Adobe Creative Suite, Digital Advertising

    - **Business & Finance:** Financial Modeling, Excel, Data Analysis, Project Management, Microsoft Office Suite, PowerPoint, Business Acumen, Strategic Planning

- **Soft Skills:** Communication, Teamwork, Problem Solving, Adaptability, Leadership, Critical Thinking, Time Management, Customer Service

o **Recommendations:** A written recommendation is gold. Ask a professor, a former manager, or a club advisor. These are genuine testimonials that add significant credibility.

- *Strategy:* Reach out to individuals who know your work well and provide them with specific examples of your contributions to highlight. Make it easy for them to write a strong recommendation.

- *Example Request:* "Dear Professor Smith, I hope you're doing well. I'm actively building my LinkedIn profile for internship applications, and I was hoping you might be willing to write a brief recommendation based on my performance in your 'Introduction to Data Structures' course. I'd be grateful if you could highlight my work on the final coding project, where I developed a unique algorithm to optimize search efficiency, and perhaps touch upon my collaborative approach in group assignments. Your endorsement would mean a lot as I pursue roles in software development."

⚙ ACTIVITY: YOUR LINKEDIN PROFILE OVERHAUL

STEP 1:

Update your headshot and create a custom banner.

STEP 2:

Write a keyword-rich, aspirational headline.

STEP 3:

Draft your 'About' section using the three-paragraph structure.

STEP 4:

Add one significant academic or personal project to the 'Projects' section.

STEP 5:

Customize your URL to linkedin.com/in/yourname.

THE BOTTOM LINE

Your LinkedIn profile is more than just an online resume; it's your professional storefront. A strategic, 'All-Star' profile is essential for attracting opportunities. Invest the time to build every piece of your profile to be a magnet for that search, and you'll transform this platform into your most powerful networking and job-landing tool.

PART III :
PUTTING YOURSELF OUT THERE:
HOW TO TALK TO PEOPLE AND ACE
THE AUDITION

It's time to move from online applications to real human conversations. Here's your playbook for networking, career fairs, and interviews.

PUTTING YOUR PROFILE TO WORK: NETWORKING & ENGAGEMENT ON LINKEDIN

An 'All-Star' profile? That's a new car in the garage. Looks great, but it won't move until you turn the engine on and drive. Engaging on LinkedIn is how you drive.

The LinkedIn algorithm rewards activity. When you're active, your profile shows up in more places, more often. More importantly, it shows recruiters that you are passionate and curious, qualities that don't show up on a static resume.

THE ART OF THE VALUE-ADD COMMENT

A generic comment like "Great post!" is invisible. Your goal is to write comments that make people think, "That's a great point."

- **The A-V-A Formula:**
  - o **Acknowledge:** Start by highlighting a specific point from the post.
  - o **Value:** Add your own perspective or share a related insight.

o **Ask:** Wrap up with an open-ended question to spark discussion.

- **Examples of Value-Add Comments:**

  o *On a post about new AI trends in marketing:* "This is a fascinating breakdown of how AI is shaping consumer engagement! I'm particularly interested in how smaller businesses can leverage these tools without a huge budget. Have you seen any impactful low-cost AI applications for local brands?"

  o *On a post from a company about a recent sustainability initiative:* "It's inspiring to see [Company Name] taking such concrete steps towards environmental responsibility. I recently researched corporate sustainability practices in my Environmental Studies class, and your approach to [specific detail] truly stands out. What do you think is the biggest challenge in implementing large-scale green initiatives?"

  o *On a post sharing an article about effective leadership in tech:* Your point about the importance of empathy in leadership really resonated with me. In my experience leading a student project team, actively listening to diverse perspectives significantly improved our problem-solving. What's one unexpected quality you've found crucial for leading innovation?"

CREATING YOUR OWN CONTENT (THE ULTIMATE ADVANTAGE)

Posting your own content establishes you as a creator, not just a consumer. It shows initiative, deep thinking, and a willingness to share knowledge, all highly valued professional traits.

- **Simple, Low-Stress Content Ideas for Students:**

  o Share a key takeaway from a class. Don't just say "Learned about marketing." Share a specific concept that intrigued you and why.

  o Post about a project you completed. Even a small personal coding project or a research paper can be highlighted.

  o Reflect on a volunteer event or workshop. What did you learn? How did it impact you?

  o Share an interesting article or industry news piece and add your unique perspective. What questions did it raise for you?

  o **Example Content Posts:**

    ▪ *A quick reflection:* "Just finished a fascinating lecture on the psychology of decision-making. It really got me thinking about how subtle cues influence consumer choices. Excited to explore this more in my upcoming marketing research project! #ConsumerBehavior #Psychology #Marketing"

    ▪ *A project showcase:* "Proud to share a small Python script I developed to automate data cleaning for my personal finance tracking. It's amazing how much time simple automation can save! Definitely looking forward to tackling more complex data challenges. #Python #DataScience #Automation"

    ▪ *An event takeaway:* "Spent Saturday volunteering at the local animal shelter's adoption event. It was a powerful reminder of the impact of community outreach. Unexpectedly got to flex some organizational skills helping manage registrations! #Volunteer #CommunityService #EventManagement"

THE OUTREACH PLAYBOOK: THE INFORMATIONAL INTERVIEW

Your goal on LinkedIn is to turn digital connections into real relationships. The informational interview (a 15-minute conversation to ask for advice, not a job) is your primary tool. It's about gathering insights and building genuine rapport.

- **The 'Who to Connect With' Ladder:**

  o **Level 1 (Inner Circle):** Connect with everyone you know: professors, classmates, family friends, former managers. Your existing network is your first and most accessible resource.

  o **Level 2 (Warm Network - Alumni):** This is your secret weapon. Use your University's 'Alumni' tab on LinkedIn. Filter by company, industry, or even location. Alumni are often incredibly willing to help fellow graduates.

  o **Level 3 (Target List):** Find 'Campus Recruiters' or 'University Recruiters' at your dream companies. They are literally paid to connect with students like you. Also, identify people in roles you aspire to.

  o **Level 4 (Professional Organizations):** Join relevant LinkedIn groups or follow professional associations in your target industry. This can open doors to broader networks and events.

- **The Art of the Connection Request: Never Use the Default**

  o A personalized message drastically increases your acceptance rate. Always include *why* you want to connect.

  o *For an Alumnus:* "Hi [Name], I'm a fellow [Your Major] at [Your University] (Class of [Your Expected Grad Year]) and found your profile while exploring careers at [Their Company]. Your work in [mention something specific from their profile, e.g., 'digital marketing'] really resonated with me. I'd love to connect and briefly hear about your experience. Go [Mascot]!"

  o *For a Recruiter:* "Hi [Name], I'm a [Your Major] student at [Your University] with a passion for [Industry, e.g., 'sustainable technology']. I've been following [Their Company]'s innovative work in [mention a specific initiative or product] and am actively seeking an internship for [Summer Year]. I'd be grateful to connect and learn more about opportunities for students."

  o *For someone in a target role (no direct connection):* "Hi [Name], I'm a [Your Major] student at [Your University] aspiring to a career in [Their Field]. I came across your profile and was particularly impressed by your experience with [specific project / skill from their profile]. I'd be honored to connect and potentially ask for a few minutes of your time to learn more about your career path at [Their Company]."

- **Following Up Gracefully:**

  o If your connection request is accepted, send a thank you message.

o If you requested an informational interview, propose a few specific times or ask what time works best for the other person. Be flexible and respectful of their schedule.

o Always send a thank-you note *after* an informational interview, reiterating what you learned and expressing your gratitude.

⚙ ACTIVITY: THE 3X3 CONNECTION CHALLENGE

STEP 1: IDENTIFY YOUR TARGETS:

Choose **three** companies you would love to intern for.

STEP 2: FIND YOUR ALUMNI:

Using the LinkedIn Alumni Tool, find **three** alumni at each of your three target companies (for a total of nine contacts).

STEP 3: DRAFT YOUR OUTREACH:

Pick one person from your list. Using the templates, draft a personalized connection request and a follow-up message asking for an informational interview.

INSIDER INSIGHT: THE POWER OF A GENUINE CONNECTION

The true power of LinkedIn lies not just in having a profile, but in actively engaging and building real relationships. Personalize your requests, engage with content thoughtfully, and look for opportunities to offer help. That's how you cultivate genuine interactions that lead to advice and opportunities.

THE BOTTOM LINE

Your LinkedIn profile is your foundation, but your active networking and engagement are the engines that drive opportunity. By consistently engaging with relevant content, sending personalized requests, and seeking opportunities to offer value, you transform your LinkedIn experience from a static resume into a dynamic network that can open doors to your dream internship.

YOUR BS DETECTOR: HOW TO SPOT FAKE JOBS AND PHONY RECRUITERS

Let's talk about the job hunt's dark side. You've sent what feels like a million applications into the internet's black hole. You're losing track. The initial excitement? Faded, replaced by deafening inbox silence. You're tired. Anxious. Desperate for a win.

Then, it happens. An email lands in your inbox.

SUBJECT: URGENT HIRING: REMOTE DATA ENTRY ASSISTANT - $45 / HOUR!

Your heart leaps. $45 an hour? To work from your dorm room? This is it! This is the one!

This is the story of Josh, a student I worked with. He jumped on it. The 'recruiter' conducted an entire interview over a messaging app, hired him on the spot, and then came the catch. They were going to mail him a check for $3,000. He was supposed to deposit it, keep $500 as his first week's pay, and then wire the remaining $2,500 to their 'equipment vendor' to pay for a new work laptop.

Luckily, Josh called me before he sent the money. That check was a fake. It would have bounced a few days after he wired *his own real money* away, leaving his account overdrawn by $2,500 and the 'recruiter' gone forever.

Josh almost fell for one of the oldest scams in the book. Scammers prey on your enthusiasm, your inexperience, and your anxiety. Your job is to make their life difficult. This chapter is your personal scam detector.

THE SCAMMER'S PLAYBOOK: THE BIG RED FLAGS

Scammers are lazy. They use the same plays over and over. Once you know what to look for, they become glaringly obvious.

- **The Offer is Too Good to Be True.** This is the #1 sign. An insane hourly wage for a simple, entry-level remote job with no interview? Forty dollars per hour to be a 'personal assistant' and read emails? Come on. If it sounds like a dream, it's probably a nightmare.

- **The Communication is Sloppy and Unprofessional.** Read the emails carefully. Are they full of typos, strange grammar, or overly urgent language ("You must act NOW!")? Is the email coming from a Gmail or Yahoo address instead of a corporate domain (e.g., jane.doe@company.com)? Legitimate recruiters take pride in their professionalism.

- **The Interview Process is Weird.** This is a huge one. A real company will, at some point, want to see and talk to you. Scammers hide.

o **Red Flag:** The *entire* interview process is conducted over a messaging app like Signal, Telegram, or even Google Chat.

o **Green Flag:** The process involves a phone screen and, critically, a video interview with a real person whose face you can see.

- **They Ask YOU for Money. Read this sentence three times: A legitimate company will NEVER, EVER ask you to pay them for a job.** They will not ask you to pay for training, a background check, or equipment. If the words 'wire,' 'Zelle,' 'gift card,' or 'processing fee' ever come up, it is a 100% scam. End of story.

- **They Ask for Sensitive Info too Soon.** You should not be providing your Social Security number, bank account details, or a copy of your driver's license until you have signed a formal offer letter and are filling out official HR paperwork (like an I-9 or W-4 form). A request for this information during an initial interview is a massive red flag.

- **The Job Description is Super Vague.** Real job postings have specific duties, qualifications, and responsibilities. Scam postings are often vague, using generic titles like 'Administrative Assistant' or 'Data Processor' with no real details about the work.

YOUR LEGITIMACY CHECKLIST: HOW TO VERIFY AN OPPORTUNITY

Okay, so you responded to a job posting that seems pretty good, and you don't see any major red flags. Awesome. Now it's time to be a detective. Your motto is: **Trust, but verify.**

- **Google Everything.** Search the company's name + the word 'scam.' Search the name of the recruiter who contacted you. You'd be surprised what you find.

- **Go to the Official Company Website.** Do not use the link in the email. Go to Google and find the company's real, official website. Does it look professional? Is the job they contacted you about listed on their official 'Careers' page? If it's not on their official site, it's probably not a real job.

- **Stalk Them on LinkedIn.** Does the company have a professional LinkedIn page with a history of posts and a list of real employees? Find the recruiter who contacted you. Do they have a profile? Does it look real, with a photo, a job history, and connections? If the recruiter has a brand-new profile with 12 connections, be suspicious.

- **Insist on a Video Call.** If you're in the interview process, simply say, "Great, I'm looking forward to our next conversation. Could you please send a video meeting link?" A scammer will often make excuses or disappear. A real company will have no problem with this.

- **Trust Your Gut.** This is the most important rule of all. If something feels off, if the process feels rushed, if the person is being pushy, listen to that little voice in your head. It's better to be safe and walk away from a potentially weird situation than to ignore your instincts and get burned.

💡 INSIDER INSIGHT: THE INTERVIEW THAT WASN'T

I talked to a student named David who was excited about an 'Operations Coordinator' role. The recruiter was professional via email. The company website looked real. Then came the interview invitation: a calendar invite to a Google Hangouts *chat*. No video link.

David joined the chat, and the 'hiring manager' started typing questions. It felt weird. Impersonal. He couldn't hear their voice or see their face. He felt like he was talking to a chatbot. Halfway through, he typed, "This feels a bit unusual. To make sure we're making a good connection, would you be open to hopping on a quick video call instead?"

The person on the other end immediately got defensive, saying this was their standard process. David's gut screamed "NOPE." He politely typed, "I appreciate your time, but I don't think this is the right fit for me. I'm going to withdraw my application." He closed the window and blocked them. He never found out for sure if it was a scam, but it doesn't matter. He trusted his gut, refused to participate in a process that felt wrong, and protected himself. That's a win.

⚙️ACTIVITY: RUN A LEGITIMACY DRILL

STEP 1: FIND A REAL JOB POSTING:

Go to the official careers page of a well-known company you admire (e.g., FedEx, Marriott, a major charity, or any national brand).

STEP 2: FIND THE 'RECRUITER':

Now go on LinkedIn and find a real recruiter or HR person who works at that company.

STEP 3: ANALYZE THE EVIDENCE:

Look at the difference between the real job posting and a potential scam. Notice the detailed description. Look at the recruiter's professional, established profile—their photo, their connections, their work history.

- *This five-minute exercise trains your brain to recognize what's real, making it much easier to spot what's fake.*

THE BOTTOM LINE

The job hunt is exciting. It should be. But in 2025, you have to be your own security guard. Scammers are banking on you being so excited about an offer that you stop asking critical questions. Don't let them be right. The single most important takeaway is this: **Money should only ever flow from the employer to you. Never the other way around.**

Apply with confidence, verify with diligence, and always, always trust your gut. You've got this.

YOUR HIGHLIGHT REEL: HOW TO TELL YOUR STORY (AND GET A CALLBACK)

Picture this: a career fair. A giant, open casting call. The room buzzes, 10 degrees too warm. You're in line to meet the 'casting director' (a recruiter) from your dream company. Heart pounding. One shot. You finally get to the front, offer a slightly sweaty handshake, and they smile. Then the director says, "Action!" or, in this case, the five words you've been dreading all day:

"So, tell me about yourself."

This is your screen test. Poof. Your mind goes blank. Every line you rehearsed, and every accomplishment you've ever had, evaporates into the stale air of the convention center.

What happens in the next 60 seconds is your audition. You don't have time to show them your entire filmography. You need a killer movie trailer. You need your story. Forget the term 'elevator pitch'; you're a storyteller. Your goal isn't to close a deal; it's to get a callback. It's to make the director lean in and say, "That's interesting, I want to see more."

YOUR STORY IS THE FULL-COLOR HIGHLIGHT REEL

Here's the deal: your resume is an old, black-and-white film. It's important, it sets the scene, and it lists the characters: your GPA, your major, and your job titles. It tells the basic plot. But it's flat, silent, and grainy.

Your story is the moment that movie bursts into glorious Technicolor. It's the full-color, widescreen, surround-sound highlight reel of your best moments. It's where you show your passion, your grit, and the 'why' behind the work you do. Casting directors see hundreds of films a day. They all start to blur together. Your job is to be the one they remember in full color.

💡 INSIDER INSIGHT: STORIES MAKE STARS

I remember asking my campus recruiting team (the casting directors) about a big career fair. When I asked if anyone stood out, they didn't mention a single GPA. They pitched me the trailers for the students they loved. One said, "Oh, you have to meet Sarah. Her highlight reel is about building an app to help her classmates find volunteer opportunities. She just lit up when she talked about it." Another said, "There was this guy, Michael, whose whole story was about his obsession with our new distribution centers. He had clearly watched our 'behind-the-scenes' footage and had ideas." Their stories made them stars.

DIRECTING YOUR 60-SECOND STORY: A FOUR-PART SCRIPT

Building your trailer is simple. You just need to script these four key scenes and make sure they flow together.

PART ONE: THE OPENING SCENE (WHO YOU ARE)

Every movie needs a clear opening. This is your title card. State your name, university, year, and major. Deliver it with the confident energy of a star walking onto the set.

- **The Shot:** "Hi, I'm Sarah Jones, a junior at the University of Tennessee studying Computer Science."

PART TWO: THE PLOT & MOTIVATION (YOUR PASSION + YOUR PROOF)

This is the heart of your film's plot. This is where you reveal your character's motivation. Don't just list your skills; that's the boring B-roll footage. Connect your passion (your character's motivation) with proof (the action scene that shows them doing it).

- **Generic B-Roll:** "I have skills in Python and Java."
- **The Feature Film:** "I'm really passionate about using technology to solve everyday problems (the motivation). For example, I recently

taught myself how to build a small web app that helps students on my campus track their volunteer hours (the action scene)."

PART THREE: THE SEQUEL (WHERE YOU'RE GOING)

A great trailer always hints at what's next. You're not just a character in a finished film; you're the star of a potential franchise. Show them you have a vision for your next chapter.

- **The Final Scene:** "So now I'm eager to take those problem-solving skills to a larger-scale production and learn from seasoned directors and a creative team."

PART FOUR: THE SPECIAL EDITION (MAKING IT ABOUT THEM)

This is the 'Director's Cut' bonus feature that makes the audience feel special. It's one sentence that shows you didn't just wander into any movie theater; you came specifically to see *their* film.

- **The Post-Credits Scene:** " ... and that's why I was so excited to talk to you today. I'm a huge fan of your studio's work, especially the new accessibility features you developed for Android. That's the kind of epic story I'd love to be a part of."

EDITING FOR YOUR AUDIENCE

A great director knows you don't show the same cut of the film to everyone. You edit for your audience.

- **The Recruiter (The Studio Executive):** They have a problem they need to solve (an open role). Cut your trailer to be action-packed. Emphasize your Proof (your skills and results) and how it solves their problem.

- **The Alum at a Mixer (The Award-Winning Director):** They aren't casting right now. Your goal is to get their wisdom. Edit your trailer to focus on your Passion and The Sequel. Ask for their advice on your character's next move.

- **A Peer (A Fellow Actor):** Keep it casual. Find common ground. "Hey, you're a marketing major too? Cool. I've been doing some 'indie films' managing social media for a club … "

⚙ ACTIVITY: YOUR DIRECTOR'S PLAYBOOK

A script is useless until the actor performs it. Time for your screen test.

STEP ONE: WRITE YOUR SCRIPT

Using the four-part structure, draft your 30-60 second trailer. Break it down scene by scene.

- **The Opening Scene (Who You Are):**

- **The Plot & Motivation (Your Passion + Proof):**

- **The Sequel (Where You're Going):**

- **The Special Edition (Use a Real Target Company / Studio):**

STEP TWO: THE RE-EDIT CHALLENGE

Outline how you'd re-edit your trailer for these two different 'screenings':

- **Audience One: The Recruiter.** You have 45 seconds. They're casting for a 'Data Analyst Intern.' Which scenes do you shorten? Which action sequence do you highlight?

- **Audience Two: The Alumni Mixer.** You're talking to a VP who isn't casting. How do you edit your trailer to be less about 'hire me' and more about 'advise me'?

STEP THREE: THE SCREEN TEST

Find a friend or family member. I know it feels weird, but every great actor rehearses.

- **Set the Scene:** Tell them they are a casting director, and you have 60 seconds to audition.

- **"Action!":** Start a timer. Deliver your lines. Make eye contact.

- **"Cut!":** Get feedback. Ask them: Was it believable? Was it compelling? What's the one scene you remember most?

- **Do Another Take.** Use their notes. The more takes you do, the less it feels like you're reading a script and the more it just feels like your story.

THE BOTTOM LINE

You might be reading this thinking, "That's great, but my life isn't a block-buster. It's a low-budget indie film. My 'action scene' was getting a B- on a group project. My 'craft services' job was at a pizza place."

Listen to me: Some of the best, most memorable films are low-budget indies. Why? Because they have heart. They have a compelling story. They have an authentic character that the audience connects with.

Your story isn't about pretending to be a big-budget superhero. It's about finding the compelling narrative in the film you've actually lived. The accounting student whose trailer was about her love for escape rooms got the part because her story was authentic and interesting. She showed character.

The goal is not to deliver a slick, over-produced, special-effects-laden pitch. The goal is to show a 60-second highlight reel that is so genuinely *you* that the casting director can't help but say, "I see the potential. I want to see more."

Find your story. Rehearse your lines. Own your role. It's the performance they'll remember.

THE RESOURCES YOU'RE ALREADY PAYING FOR (BUT PROBABLY NOT USING)

We've honed your resume, optimized LinkedIn, and crafted your story. Now, activate your most powerful built-in secret weapons: your university's Career Center, student groups, and global Alumni Network.

Most students drastically underuse these resources. They might visit the Career Center once for a quick resume check but leave a goldmine of opportunities untouched. Think of these services not as simple support systems but as your exclusive, members-only club for career advancement. Actively using them isn't just helpful; it's a serious competitive advantage over students at other schools who don't have this same support.

YOUR CAREER CENTER: MORE THAN JUST RESUME REVIEWS

The biggest mistake students make is thinking the Career Center is just a place to get a quick resume check. That's like using a supercomputer as a calculator. A modern Career Center is a full-service strategic command post for your internship search.

- **Go Beyond the Basic Mock Interview:** Don't just ask for a 'mock interview.' Be specific. When you book an appointment, apply your research. Say, "I have an upcoming behavioral interview for a marketing internship at a CPG company. Could I schedule a mock interview with a counselor who has experience in that area so I can practice my STAR Method answers with interviewing skills?" This shows you're a serious candidate and allows them to provide tailored, high-impact feedback.

- **Access Exclusive Job Boards:** Your Career Center's job portal (like Handshake) is a curated list of employers who *want* to hire from your school. The competition is a fraction of what you'll face on global sites. Make checking this a weekly habit.

- **Master Employer Information Sessions:** When a company holds an info session on campus, it's an audition. Arrive early, stay late, and apply your Chapter Three research by preparing one thoughtful question you couldn't find the answer to online.

- **Your Go-To Question:** "Thank you for the presentation. For the students here today who are really serious about joining [Company Name], what's one thing you'd recommend they do after this session to be a stronger candidate for the summer internship program?"

- **Unlock Salary and Offer Negotiation Advice:** If you get an offer, your career counselor can be an invaluable guide. They often have data on what other students have been offered and can coach you on how to professionally negotiate.

STUDENT GROUPS: YOUR REAL-WORLD TRAINING GROUND

The clubs you join are more than just a social outlet; they are your first opportunity to *apply* your skills in a professional context.

- **Seek Leadership Roles:** Don't just pay dues. Run the show. Treasurer of the Finance Club? Social Media Chair for Marketing? These aren't just titles. They're concrete, quantifiable wins for your resume. Turn a club into a proving ground.

- **Attend Sponsor Events:** These aren't casual mixers. Big corporations back these clubs for a reason. Exclusive events. Insider workshops. This is your fast pass to recruiters from your target companies. Show up. Network. Get seen.

- **Build Your Portfolio:** Club projects, designing flyers, managing budgets, and running events are your tangible, real-world examples. This isn't just busywork. These are the stories you'll use in every interview. This is your proof.

YOUR ALUMNI NETWORK: THE ULTIMATE ADVOCATES

Your university has thousands of alumni working at every major company, in every industry, all over the world. This isn't a cold network; it's a warm one, bonded by a shared experience. Most alumni *want* to help students from their alma mater. Your job is to make it easy for them to help you.

- **The LinkedIn Alumni Tool Method:** Your career center can give you access to an official alumni database, but your most powerful tool is LinkedIn. Navigate to your university's official LinkedIn page, click the 'Alumni' tab, and use the filters to find exactly who you're looking for based on your target company and role research.

- **The Art of the 'Warm' Outreach:** The goal of your first message is to ask for a 15-minute informational interview to hear their story and get advice. Always lead with your shared connection.

- **LinkedIn Connection Request Template:** "Hi [Alum's Name], I'm a fellow [Your Major] at [Your University] and saw you work at [Their Company]. I'm inspired by your career path and would be grateful for the chance to connect. Go [Mascots]!"

- **Follow-Up Message Template (After they connect):** "Hi [Alum's Name], Thank you for connecting. As a [Your Year] student studying [Your Major], I'm currently exploring career paths in [Their Industry]. I find your work at [Their Company] especially inspiring. If you have 15 minutes in the next few weeks, I'd be grateful for the chance to hear about your experience and any advice you might have for a student hoping to follow a similar path."

- **Conduct a Professional Informational Interview:** When an alum agrees to chat, be prepared. Ask thoughtful questions like, "Can you tell me about your career path from [Your University] to your current role?" and "What skills do you think are most crucial for success in [Their Field] today?" End with the powerful question: "Is there anyone else in your network you think would be helpful for me to talk to?"

⚙ ACTIVITY: THE CAREER QUEST TRIPLE-THREAT

The most effective students don't just use their campus resources; they combine them like power-ups in a video game to create a winning strategy. This activity challenges you to move beyond a simple to-do list and create a multipronged quest to unlock an opportunity at your dream company.

Your Mission: To use all three resources (Career Center, Student Groups, and Alumni Network) to gather clues, build your skills, and make a powerful connection at a single target company.

STEP ONE: SELECT YOUR MAIN QUEST

Every great adventure needs a goal. Select **ONE** company from your list of dream employers. This company is the objective of your main quest.

- **My Main Quest (Target Company):** _____

STEP TWO: THE CAREER CENTER BRIEFING

Think of the Career Center as your mission control. It's where you get the map and the key intelligence before you start the game.

- **Action Item:** Schedule a 15-minute meeting with a career adviser. In your meeting request, state your quest objective: "I am targeting an internship at [Your Target Company] and would like to strategize the best way to approach them." Ask these specific questions to gather clues:

o Does our university have any special recruiting connections or contacts at this company?

o Has this company historically attended our career fairs or info sessions?

o Can you help me practice a 30-second pitch specifically for a role at this company?

- **Clues Gathered:** _____

STEP THREE: THE STUDENT GROUP SIDE QUEST

Your student group is a valuable side quest that can grant you a special power-up (like a new skill or a direct contact).

- **Action Item:** Identify one student group you are in (or could join) that is relevant to your target company's industry (e.g., Finance Society, Marketing Club, Society of Women Engineers). Then, investigate:

  o Is [Your Target Company] a corporate sponsor of this group?

  o Are there any upcoming events (workshops, speaker series) featuring employees from this company? This could be a hidden door!

  o Can you take on a leadership role (e.g., corporate relations chair) that would let you earn 'experience points' by reaching out to the company?

- **Power-Up Unlocked:** _____

STEP FOUR: THE ALUMNI NETWORK GUIDE

In every great quest, the hero finds a seasoned guide who knows the way. Your alumni network is full of them. This is where you use the clues you've gathered to connect with an insider.

- **Action Item:** Use the LinkedIn Alumni Tool to find **two** alumni who currently work at [Your Target Company]. One should be a recent graduate (a fellow adventurer who just completed the level) and one should be more experienced (a high-level guide).

- **Draft Your Message:** Using the template from this chapter, draft a personalized connection request for the recent graduate. Weave in the clues you gathered from your other quests.

  o **Example:** "Hi [Alum's Name], I'm a fellow [Major] at [University] and was so inspired by your career path. I learned from our Career Center that [Target Company] is a top destination for our grads, and I'd be grateful for the chance to hear about your experience on the inside."

- **My Drafted Message:** _____

By completing this quest, you've done more than just use three resources. You've created a smart, focused campaign that proves you're not just another player, you're a strategist who knows how to solve the puzzle and win the game.

☀ INSIDER INSIGHT: THE 'HIDDEN GEM' STUDENT

I once mentored a student who, despite not having a stellar GPA, landed a top-tier internship. How? I encouraged her to fully use her school's career services by attending every workshop, using mock interviews to perfect her stories, and networking relentlessly through alumni events and LinkedIn. She built such strong relationships with several managers at her dream company, that when an opening came up there, multiple alumni at the company championed her candidacy internally. It wasn't about grades or a flawless resume; it was about maximizing every resource and demonstrating incredible drive.

THE BOTTOM LINE

Your university isn't just a place where you rack up student loan debt and perfect the art of pulling all-nighters. The Career Center, student groups, and the alumni network: most students are just letting these valuable resources go to waste. You bought the concert ticket, but you're standing outside. Stop it. These aren't just extras; they're your strategic edge, the cheat codes to landing that dream internship. Every connection you don't make, and every resource you ignore, is an opportunity wasted. Become an active investor in your future. The resources are there; go use them.

STOP APPLYING, START CONNECTING

You found it: the perfect internship posting. Resume tailored, killer cover letter written, and 'submit' hit. Then ... nothing. Crickets. It's one of the most frustrating feelings in the internship search. You know you're qualified, but you're stuck in a massive digital line with thousands of other students, all hoping to get noticed.

What if I told you there was a backdoor? A way to bypass the line and get your resume seen by a real person? This isn't about a secret trick; it's about a fundamental shift in strategy. The most successful students don't just apply for jobs; they connect with the people who do the hiring. In today's market, your network isn't just a nice-to-have; it's your single most powerful advantage.

THE INFORMATIONAL INTERVIEW: YOUR ULTIMATE BACKDOOR PASS

A referral from a current employee is the most powerful power-up you can get. A referred candidate is over four times more likely to get an offer than someone who just applies online. The primary tool for building the relationships that lead to these referrals is the informational interview.

Let's be clear: this is a 15-minute conversation to ask for advice, not a job. It's a low-pressure chat where you get to learn from an insider, and they get to see your passion and professionalism up close.

THE FIVE-PHASE PLAN

PHASE ONE: IDENTIFY YOUR CONTACT

Use LinkedIn to identify an alum from your university who now works at a target company; this is your warmest possible connection. They've walked in your shoes, and most are happy to help a fellow alum.

PHASE TWO: DO YOUR RECONNAISSANCE

Spend at least 10 minutes researching them. Read their LinkedIn profile carefully. What does their career path look like? Have they published any articles? Find one specific detail that genuinely interests you. This shows you've done your homework.

PHASE THREE: CRAFT THE 'WARM' OUTREACH

Send a thoughtful, personalized connection request, then follow up with a message once they accept.

- **Example: LinkedIn Connection Request (Alum):** "Hi Ms. Davis, I'm a marketing student at the University of Memphis and was so impressed by your career path to FedEx. I'd love to connect and learn a bit about your experience. Go Tigers!"

- **Follow-Up Message (After They Connect):**

  Subject: University of Memphis Student Seeking Advice

  Hi Ms. Davis,

  Thank you so much for connecting. I'm a junior here at University of Memphis and am passionate about building a career in logistics marketing. I noticed on your profile that you led the 'Deliver Today' campaign, which I followed closely; it was brilliant.

  If you have a spare 15 minutes in the coming weeks for a brief chat, I'd be incredibly grateful for any advice you could share with a student hoping to break into the industry.

  Best regards,

  [Your Name]

PHASE FOUR: PREPARE YOUR KEY QUESTIONS

This is not just a casual chat; it's a fact-finding mission. Have three to four thoughtful questions ready that go beyond the basics.

- "What has been the most surprising or unexpected part of your role at [Company Name]?"

- "What skills do you see becoming more important in your industry over the next few years?"

- "What's the best piece of advice you have for a student trying to land their first great internship in this field?"

PHASE FIVE: THE FLAWLESS FOLLOW-UP

Send a personalized thank-you note within 24 hours. Reference a specific insight or piece of advice they shared. This reinforces the positive connection and shows you truly valued their time.

INSIDER INSIGHT: HOW THE INFORMATIONAL INTERVIEW BECOMES THE OPPORTUNITY

I've seen this work firsthand. A student connected with one of our senior VPs for an informational chat. The VP was so impressed by the student's thoughtful questions and genuine curiosity that when an unexpected internship opening came up on his team a few weeks later, he immediately told my team, 'I know exactly who we need for this.' That student never submitted an online application for that role; the opportunity was created for them through a well-nurtured connection.

INFILTRATE THE INDUSTRY: WHERE TO FIND YOUR PEOPLE

So, where do you find these people to connect with? You need to go where the professionals are.

- **Join Professional Associations:** Don't just lurk. Become a student member. Think HR, Marketing, or your area of special interest. These aren't just clubs; they're access points: cheap entry to exclusive events and insider directories. This is where the real players hang out.

- **Attend Local Meetups & Events:** Get off your couch. Platforms like Meetup.com and Eventbrite are your intel. Find your tribe, whether that's Seattle UX or NYC Python. These informal gatherings are prime hunting grounds for genuine connections with passionate pros.

Leverage Your Professors: They've got the contacts. They know the players. Show genuine interest in a specific area during office hours. Then, hit them up. Ask for their guidance on companies or individuals. Your instructors can open doors.

⚙ ACTIVITY: YOUR PROACTIVE SEARCH MISSION

STEP ONE: THE INFORMATIONAL INTERVIEW DRAFT:

- Identify one alumnus on LinkedIn who works at one of your target companies.

- Using the example script above, draft a personalized follow-up message asking for a 15-minute chat.

- Save this draft in a document so it's ready when you need it.

STEP TWO: LOCAL EVENT RECONNAISSANCE:

- Use Meetup.com or a similar platform to find at least one professional event or group meeting in your field of interest happening in your area within the next two months.

- Note the event's date, location, and any sponsoring companies.

STEP THREE: THE PROFESSOR APPROACH:

- Identify one professor in your department with relevant industry connections.

- Write down a clear two-sentence script you can use during the instructor's office hours to ask for advice.

THE BOTTOM LINE

The students who land the best internships are rarely the ones who only apply online. They are the ones who are proactive, strategic, and courageous enough to build real human connections. It takes more effort, but the payoff is enormous. Stop waiting for opportunities to come to you. Go out and create them.

MAKING CONNECTIONS THAT COUNT: A GUIDE TO CAREER FAIRS & EVENTS

You've built your target list, and you know the kinds of roles you're looking for. Now it's time to move from online research to the real world. It's time to meet the recruiters.

Career fairs and hiring events are your chance to make a memorable first impression and turn a digital application into a human connection. But let's be honest, career fairs can be overwhelming. A crowded room, long lines, and the pressure to say the perfect thing can make even the most confident student nervous.

To truly stand out, you need to approach these events not as a passive attendee, but as a strategic player. This chapter is your game plan.

BEFORE THE EVENT: PREPARATION IS YOUR SUPERPOWER

The key to a successful career fair experience lies in diligent preparation. Students who truly excel at these these events are those who invest time in doing their homework, rather than simply showing up and wandering aimlessly.

- **Do Your Reconnaissance:** Before stepping foot into the event, acquire the official list of participating companies. This list is your blueprint. Cross-reference it with your personal 'hit list' of desired organizations and meticulously identify your top five to ten priority companies. These are the companies you absolutely want to connect with.

- **Go Beyond the Homepage:** For each of your top target companies, dedicate at least 15 minutes to in-depth research. Don't stop at their homepage; delve into their 'News' or 'Press Releases' sections. What recent projects have they launched? Are there any exciting new initiatives or products? Furthermore, understand their core values and company culture. Do they prioritize innovation, collaboration, or community involvement? This deeper understanding will not only impress recruiters but will also fuel the intelligent, insightful questions you'll be able to ask, demonstrating genuine interest and a proactive approach.

- **Polish Your Pitch:** Your 60-second personal story, often referred to as an 'elevator pitch,' is a critical component of your arsenal. This concise yet compelling summary of who you are, what you're passionate about, and what you're looking for should be practiced repeatedly until it flows naturally and confidently. It should highlight your relevant skills and experiences and articulate why you're a strong candidate for an internship with their company.

- **Prepare Your Materials:** Ensure you have at least 15 copies of your tailored resume. Each resume should be updated to reflect the specific internship opportunities you're targeting and presented immaculately in a professional-looking folder to prevent creasing or damage. In addition, bring a small notebook and a reliable pen. These will be invaluable for jotting down key details, names, and follow-up notes immediately after each conversation, helping you remember important information and personalize your thank-you notes later.

- **Plan Your Outfit:** Your attire speaks volumes before you even utter a word. Dress professionally and conservatively. This demonstrates respect for the recruiters, the company, and the opportunity at hand. When in doubt, it's always better to overdress than to underdress. A well-fitting suit or business casual attire conveys seriousness and a readiness for a professional environment.

INSIDER INSIGHT: BEYOND THE BIG NAMES, YOUR DREAM INTERNSHIP MIGHT BE HIDING IN PLAIN SIGHT

While thousands of students swarm the booths for Google and Deloitte, they often overlook incredible opportunities at lesser-known industry leaders. At your next career fair, challenge yourself: take five minutes to research one company that isn't a famous logo. You might discover that at a household-name company, you'd be intern #743 on a tiny project, while at a 'hidden champion' B2B company, you could be one of 50 interns trusted to own a real project from start to finish. The best opportunities are often where the lines are shortest.

DURING THE EVENT: HOW TO MAKE EVERY CONVERSATION COUNT

- **Approach with Confidence:** Make eye contact, offer a firm handshake, and introduce yourself with your polished personal story.

- **Engage in a Real Conversation:** Don't just launch into a monologue. After your pitch, ask a thoughtful, research-based question. "I read about your new sustainability initiative. How is the marketing team involved in that?"

- **Take Notes (Afterwards):** Immediately after you walk away from a booth, jot down the recruiter's name and one key thing you discussed. This is essential for your follow-up.

- **Collect Business Cards:** Always ask for a business card. It's your ticket to a personalized follow-up.

AFTER THE EVENT: THE FOLLOW-UP THAT SEALS THE DEAL

- **Send a Thank-You Email:** Within 24 hours, send a personalized thank-you email to each recruiter you spoke with. Reference the specific detail you wrote down to refresh their memory.

- **Connect on LinkedIn:** Send a personalized LinkedIn connection request. "Hi [Name], it was great meeting you at the [University Name] career fair today. I really enjoyed our conversation about [specific topic]."

- **Follow Through:** If a recruiter told you to apply online for a specific role, do it promptly. In your thank-you email, you can even mention that you have completed the online application as they suggested.

⚙ ACTIVITY: THE 'PRE-FAIR' RESEARCH SPRINT

Goal: To equip you with specific, impressive talking points for your next career fair or networking event.

STEP ONE: PICK YOUR TOP THREE:

- Identify three companies you anticipate being at a career fair or networking event that you would genuinely love to intern for.

STEP TWO: DIVE DEEP (FIVE TO SEVEN MINUTES PER COMPANY):

- For each company, go beyond their main 'About Us' page. Look for:

  o A recent project, product launch, or major news announcement.

  o A core value or initiative that genuinely resonates with you (e.g., sustainability, innovation, or community involvement).

  o The name / title of a specific recruiter or hiring manager if you can find one via LinkedIn.

STEP THREE: CRAFT YOUR 'SMART QUESTION':

- For each of your three companies, write down one thoughtful question that incorporates your research. This question should show you've done your homework and are genuinely interested.

- **Example:** "I read about your recent expansion into the European market. How do you see the marketing team supporting that growth, particularly with digital campaigns?"

This exercise trains your brain to quickly find the details that make you sound like a prepared, serious candidate.

THE BOTTOM LINE:

Career fairs and networking events aren't just places to collect free pens; they're prime opportunities to make genuine connections that can open doors. By approaching these events with a strategic game plan: researching companies, crafting your pitch, and preparing thoughtful questions, you move beyond passively browsing to actively engaging. Follow up diligently, and you'll transform these interactions into valuable leads for your dream internship. Success at these events is about preparation, confidence, and making every connection count.

THE INTERVIEW GAUNTLET: FROM PHONE SCREEN TO FINAL ROUND

You did it. Your resume, your networking, and your preparation at the career fair paid off. You got the email. You've been invited to an interview.

Now, it's time to showcase your personality, communication skills, and critical thinking in real time. For recruiters, the interview isn't just about what you say, but how you say it, your energy, your enthusiasm, and whether you genuinely fit with the team. This chapter will give you the strategies you need to shine at every stage of the interview process.

THE FIRST HURDLE: THE PHONE SCREEN

This initial 15-30 minute call with a recruiter is a filter. Their goal is to quickly confirm your basic qualifications and assess your communication skills.

WHAT THEY'RE LOOKING FOR:

- **The Basics:** Do you meet the core requirements (graduation date, major, and work authorization)?

- **Communication Skills:** Are you clear, professional, and enthusiastic?

- **Genuine Interest:** Are you excited about *this* company, or just any company?

HOW TO SUCCEED:

- **Find a Quiet Spot:** Take the call in a place with no background noise and strong cell service.

- **Smile When You Talk:** It sounds silly, but the interviewer can hear the energy in your voice.

- **Have Your Resume Ready:** Have a copy of your resume and the job description in front of you.

- **Prepare Your 'Why':** Be ready to answer "Why are you interested in this internship?" with a specific, research-based answer.

THE MAIN EVENT: BEHAVIORAL INTERVIEWS & THE STAR METHOD

Behavioral questions are designed to see how you've handled situations in the past, which is a great predictor of how you'll perform in the future. They usually start with "Tell me about a time when … " or "Give me an example of … " This is where the **STAR Method** becomes your best friend.

STAR stands for:

- **S - Situation:** Set the scene. Briefly describe the background context of your story. (e.g., "In my marketing class, our team was assigned a major project to create a marketing plan for a local business.")

- **T - Task:** Explain your role and responsibility in that situation. (e.g., "My specific task was to lead the market research and competitive analysis.")

- **A - Action:** Describe the specific steps you took. This is the most crucial part. (e.g., "I designed a survey and interviewed 20 customers to gather insights. Then, I analyzed three key competitors to identify a gap in the market.")

- **R - Result:** Explain the outcome. Quantify it whenever possible. (e.g., "As a result, our team's final plan was projected to increase customer traffic by 15%, and we earned a 95% grade on the project.")

INSIDER INSIGHT: THE SUBTLE RED FLAGS

I often noticed subtle red flags during interviews. Candidates who kept saying 'we' instead of 'I' when describing their contributions, or who blamed others for challenges, immediately raised questions about their accountability. Your ability to clearly and confidently communicate the actions you took is what sets you apart.

THE EXPERT LEVEL: TECHNICAL & CASE INTERVIEWS

For some roles (like software engineering or consulting), you'll face specialized interviews designed to test your raw skills.

- **Technical Interviews:** These test your coding skills and understanding of concepts like algorithms and data structures.

  o **How to Prepare:** Practice coding problems on platforms like LeetCode or HackerRank. Crucially, practice explaining your thought process *out loud* as you solve a problem. Interviewers want to see how you think.

  o **Potential Pitfall:** while an AI assistant may be a great tool to *practice* your technical skills, an AI agent or interface should never be used during an interview to assist you.

- **Case Interviews:** Common in consulting, these test your structured problem-solving skills with a real-world business scenario.

  o **How to Prepare:** Learn common case frameworks, but don't be rigid. Practice breaking down complex problems and asking smart, clarifying questions before you jump to a solution.

  o **Potential Pitfall:** a common misconception about case studies is that companies conduct these to extract feel labor from candidates. In reality, it's not about how correct your answer is; it's more a forum for you to demonstrate how you think and work in real time.

YOUR AI CO-PILOT: ACING INTERVIEW PREP

As we discussed in Chapter Five, AI is a powerful co-pilot for your internship search, and nowhere is this truer than in interview preparation. Acing an interview is all about practice and preparation, and AI can be your 24/7 personal prep coach.

- **Generating Practice Questions:** Before you can practice your answers, you need to know what to expect.

  o **Prompt:** "Act as a senior recruiter at a top tech company. I am a college junior interviewing for a 'Data Analyst Internship.' Based on the attached job description, generate 10 likely behavioral interview questions and five technical questions I should prepare for."

- **Refining Your STAR Stories:** Once you've drafted a STAR story, AI can help you make it more concise and impactful.

  o **Prompt:** "Here is my answer to 'Tell me about a time you worked on a team.' Please review it using the STAR method and suggest ways to make it more concise and to better highlight the quantifiable result: [Paste your draft answer here]."

- **Simulating a Mock Interview:** This is one of the most powerful ways to use AI.

  o **Prompt:** "Let's do a mock interview. You are the hiring manager for a marketing internship. I am the student candidate. Ask me the first question. Wait for my response, and then provide constructive feedback on my answer (was it clear? did it use the STAR method?) and then ask the next question."

YOUR TURN TO INTERVIEW THEM: ASKING SMART QUESTIONS

At the end of nearly every interview, you'll hear, "Do you have any questions for us?" Your answer should never be 'No.' This is your final opportunity to show your genuine interest and to figure out if this is a place you actually want to work.

QUESTIONS THAT SHOW YOU WANT TO MAKE AN IMPACT:

- "Can you describe what a successful intern in this role will have accomplished by the end of the summer?"

- "What is the most significant challenge the team is facing right now that an intern could contribute to?"

- "How will the projects I work on directly support the team's broader goals for this quarter?"

QUESTIONS THAT PROVE YOU'VE DONE YOUR RESEARCH:

- "I read about your company's new sustainability initiative. How do you see the work of this team contributing to that goal?"

- "As the [Your Industry] industry continues to evolve with [a specific trend, e.g., the rise of generative AI], how is the team adapting its strategy?"

QUESTIONS THAT SHOW YOU ARE COACHABLE AND EAGER TO GROW:

- "What does the mentorship and feedback process look like for interns?"

- "What differentiates the interns who have been most successful here in the past from those who just met expectations?"

QUESTIONS THAT BUILD PERSONAL RAPPORT:

- (To the interviewer) "What has been your favorite project to work on here at [Company Name]?"

- "What are the most valued traits in a team member here, beyond the technical skills on the job description?"

THE POWERFUL CLOSING QUESTION:

- "Is there anything about my background or experience that gives you pause, or is there anything I could clarify for you?" (This is a confident question that gives you a final chance to address any concerns.)

⚙ACTIVITY: YOUR INTERVIEW GAME PLAN

STEP ONE: BUILD YOUR STAR BANK:

Write out three full STAR stories based on your resume's bullet points. Choose examples that showcase teamwork, problem-solving, and initiative.

STEP TWO: CREATE YOUR QUESTION ARSENAL:

Based on your research of a target company, develop three specific, insightful questions you could ask an interviewer that prove you've done your homework.

STEP THREE: RUN AN AI MOCK INTERVIEW:

Use the prompt from the AI Co-Pilot section to run a simulated interview for your target role. Copy and paste at least one of your STAR stories and ask for feedback.

THE BOTTOM LINE:

Mastering different interview formats and the STAR method is your key to confidently and effectively showcasing your skills and experiences. By understanding what recruiters are looking for in behavioral questions and practicing how to structure your responses using STAR, you'll move beyond generic answers. You will provide compelling, results-driven examples that demonstrate your value and significantly increase your chances of landing that internship offer. Preparation and practice are your superpowers in the interview room.

THE THANK-YOU NOTE THAT SEALS THE DEAL

We all know it's true. After a brain-draining interview, the absolute last thing you want to do is write a thank-you note. It feels like a chore, another box to check. You're tempted to just cross your fingers, hope for the best, and tell yourself, "They probably don't even read them."

That's a mistake. And this isn't about being polite or following some old-fashioned rule your parents told you about. This is about strategy.

Think of the thank-you note as the post-credits scene of your interview. The interview is the main movie. Most people get up and leave when the credits roll. But the best candidates, the ones who are really paying attention, know to stay for the end credit scene.

In an age of instant, lazy communication, a thoughtful, well-crafted thank-you note has become a surprisingly rare and powerful tool. Think of it this way: if you and another candidate are neck-and-neck in qualifications, the thank-you note can absolutely be the tiebreaker that tips the scales in your favor. It proves you're organized, appreciative, and genuinely interested in the opportunity. I suggest sending an individual note to every person you interact with during the interview process, specifying something specific you learned about them and the job opportunity or company. If this feels too daunting, at minimum thank the Recruiter and Hiring Manager.

THE THREE P'S OF A PERFECT THANK-YOU NOTE

The thank-you note. It's not a courtesy; it's a weapon. Here are the 'Three P's' to make it hit home:

- **Prompt:** Send that note within 24 hours. Same day is ideal. Hesitate, and it's an afterthought. Your enthusiasm? Gone.

- **Personalized:** Forget generic. Copy-pasted? Worse than nothing. Call out specific points from your conversation. Prove you were listening. Prove you're invested.

- **Professional:** Formal, yet warm. Clear subject line. Flawless grammar. Polish that closing. Email is the standard. Don't overthink it; just execute.

ANATOMY OF A STAND-OUT THANK-YOU NOTE

Follow this simple structure to craft a memorable note that reinforces your value.

THE SUBJECT LINE: BE CLEAR, NOT CUTE

A recruiter gets hundreds of emails a day. Your subject line needs to be clear and easily searchable.

- **Weak:** 'Thanks!' or 'Following up'
- **Strong:** "Thank You - [Your Name], [Role Name] Interview" or "Following up on our conversation for the Marketing Internship"

THE PERSONALIZED GREETING

Address the interviewer by name. Match the formality they used with you. If they signed their email 'Best, David,' you can greet them with 'Hi David.' If they were 'Mr. Thompson' throughout the interview, stick with that.

THE OPENING: GRATITUDE AND ENTHUSIASM

Start by thanking them for their time and immediately reiterating your strong interest in the role.

- **Example:** "Thank you again for taking the time to speak with me today about the Summer Financial Analyst internship. I truly enjoyed our conversation and came away with an even greater appreciation for the rigorous and collaborative environment at [Company Name]."

THE CONNECTION POINT (THE CORE)

This is the most important part of your note. Mention one specific thing you discussed that resonated with you. This proves you were paying attention and moves your note from generic to memorable.

- **Example:** "I was especially interested in our discussion about the team's approach to valuing emerging market equities ... " or "I especially enjoyed hearing about the team's upcoming project to redesign the mobile onboarding flow."

THE VALUE-ADD (THE GENTLE REMINDER)

Briefly and subtly connect that point back to a skill or experience you have. This isn't about bragging; it's about gently reminding them how you can contribute.

- **Example:** " ... It directly connected with the valuation models I built for my International Finance class project, and I'm confident my analytical skills would allow me to contribute meaningfully to that work."

THE CLOSING: A CONFIDENT FINISH

Express your enthusiasm for the next steps and sign off professionally with your contact information.

EMAIL VS. HANDWRITTEN NOTE: THE MODERN DILEMMA

- **Email is the Standard:** For 99% of situations, a prompt, well-written email is the best choice. It's fast, professional, and what recruiters expect.

- **The Handwritten Note (the Pro-Level Move):** In some more traditional industries (like law or some finance roles), or if you had an incredibly strong personal connection with the interviewer, a handwritten note can be a powerful touch. It stands out in a digital world.

INSIDER INSIGHT

I always carried a few blank thank-you cards with me to in-person interviews. Before I left the building, I'd sit in the lobby or a nearby coffee shop and write a thoughtful note. I brought pre-stamped envelopes so I could mail it the same day, or I would drop it off with the reception desk. While not required, I know from my own experience as a recruiter that this gesture is memorable and shows an incredible level of polish and initiative.

THANK-YOU NOTE BLUEPRINTS IN ACTION

Here are two distinct examples. Notice how the core message is the same, but the tone adapts to the likely company culture.

EXAMPLE ONE: THE CORPORATE / FORMAL ROLE (E.G., FINANCE, LAW, OR CONSULTING)

Subject: Thank You - John Miller, Summer Analyst Interview

Dear Mr. Thompson,

Thank you again for taking the time to speak with me today about the Summer Financial Analyst internship. I truly enjoyed our conversation and came away with an even greater appreciation for the rigorous and collaborative environment at [Company Name].

I was especially interested in our discussion about the team's approach to valuing emerging market equities. It directly connects with the valuation models I built for my International Finance class project, and I'm confident my analytical skills would allow me to contribute meaningfully to that work.

I'm very enthusiastic about the opportunity to join your team. Please let me know if there's any additional information I can provide.

Best regards,

John Miller

(555) 123-4567

john.miller@email.com

[Link to your LinkedIn Profile]

EXAMPLE TWO: THE TECH/CREATIVE ROLE (E.G., MARKETING, SOFTWARE ENGINEERING, OR DESIGN)

Subject: Great chatting about the UX Design Internship!

Hi Sarah,

Thank you so much for the great conversation earlier today! It was fantastic to learn more about the UX Design internship and the user-centric philosophy at [Company Name].

I especially enjoyed hearing about the team's upcoming project to redesign the mobile onboarding flow. Your emphasis on using user feedback to guide every design choice really resonated with me, as it's the same principle I applied when I developed a prototype for a campus event app last semester.

I left our conversation feeling genuinely excited about the possibility of contributing my passion for clean design and user research to your team. Looking forward to hearing about the next steps.

All the best,

Aisha Khan

(555) 987-0000

aisha.khan@email.com

[Link to your LinkedIn Profile or Portfolio]

⚙ ACTIVITY: THE 24-HOUR THANK-YOU DRILL

You can't wait until after a real interview to think about how to write a thank-you note. Let's practice now so you're ready to deploy it under pressure.

Your Mission: Imagine you just finished an interview for your ideal internship. The interviewer's name was Ali Smith, and the most interesting part of the conversation was when they described how the intern team gets to work on a real client-facing project that ships at the end of the summer.

STEP ONE: SET A TIMER FOR 15 MINUTES:

This drill simulates the real-world need to be prompt and efficient.

STEP TWO: DRAFT THE EMAIL:

Open a blank document or email draft. Using the structure and examples above, write a complete thank-you note to Ali Smith.

STEP THREE: PERSONALIZE THE 'CONNECTION POINT':

Be sure to mention the client-facing summer project and tie it directly to a skill or passion you have (for example, your drive to see your work make a real impact, or your project management experience from a class).

STEP FOUR: REVIEW AND REFINE:

Check for spelling, grammar, and tone. Does it sound appreciative and confident?

By completing this exercise, you'll have a strong template ready and more importantly, the confidence to craft a polished, personalized thank-you note when it truly counts.

THE BOTTOM LINE

The thank-you note is your chance to have the last word when everyone else has gone silent. It's the scene that proves you were listening, connects one more dot between your skills and the company's problems, and reinforces that you are the hero for the job. When a hiring manager is staring at two equal resumes, the thoughtful thank-you note is the tie-breaker. Every time.

PART IV:
YOU'RE IN! (NOW WHAT?):
OFFERS, REJECTION, AND HOW TO BE
THE INTERN THEY CAN'T LIVE WITHOUT

This is where the real world hits. How to handle offers, bounce back from rejection, and crush your internship from day one.

JUGGLING OFFERS, EXPLODING DEADLINES, AND OTHER HIGH-STAKES DECISIONS

You've done everything right. Now, the unthinkable: a decision. Perhaps a great offer from your second-choice company while your dream company still interviews. Maybe two amazing offers simultaneously. Or, the ultimate high-pressure scenario: an 'exploding offer,' a great opportunity with a terrifyingly short deadline.

This is the 'good problem to have' that every student dreams of, but it can also be incredibly stressful. How you handle this final stage of the game says a lot about your professionalism and can impact your reputation for years to come. This chapter is your playbook for navigating these high-stakes decisions with confidence and grace.

THE EXPLODING OFFER: HOW TO DEFUSE THE BOMB

You get an email or a call. You got the offer! It's exciting, the pay is good ... and then comes the kicker: "We need a decision by Friday." It's Wednesday. This is an 'exploding offer,' and it's a high-pressure tactic designed to get you to say 'yes' before you can explore other options. Your first instinct might be to panic. Don't. You have more power here than you think.

EXPRESS GRATITUDE AND ENTHUSIASM (IMMEDIATELY)

The very first thing you do is offer a sincere thanks.. This reinforces that you are a serious and appreciative candidate.

- "Thank you so much for this incredible offer! I am so excited about the possibility of joining your team and contributing to [Project Name]."

THE PROFESSIONAL AND HONEST ASK FOR AN EXTENSION.

It is completely reasonable to ask for more time to make a thoughtful decision. Frame it not as a delay tactic, but as a sign of your diligence.

- "This is a very important decision for me, and I want to give it the careful consideration it deserves. Would it be possible to have until the end of next week to give you my final answer?"

IF THEY PUSH BACK: THE TRANSPARENT FOLLOW-UP.

If they say no or hesitate, you can be a bit more transparent while still being professional.

- "I completely understand your timeline. To be fully transparent, I am in the final stages of the interview process with one other company, which I expect to wrap up early next week. Because your company is a top choice for me, I want to be able to see that process through before making my final commitment."

💡 INSIDER INSIGHT: WHY WE GIVE DEADLINES (AND WHEN WE BEND THEM)

From a recruiter's perspective, we create deadlines to keep the process moving. We have hiring goals to meet, and we can't wait forever. However, we also know that top candidates often have multiple options. When a student professionally and respectfully asks for a one-week extension because they are in the final rounds with another company, it doesn't make them look bad; it actually reinforces their value. It tells us they are in high demand. We would almost always grant a reasonable extension for a strong candidate. The students who handled this poorly were the ones who just ghosted us until the deadline, which signaled a lack of communication skills.

JUGGLING MULTIPLE OFFERS: THE ART OF THE COMPARISON

Congratulations, you're a rock star! But now you have to choose. This isn't just about comparing the hourly wage. You need to create a 'Personal Scorecard' to evaluate the offers holistically.

- **The Obvious: The Money.** What is the total compensation (hourly wage, stipends for housing, or travel)?

- **The Work Itself:** Which role seems more interesting? Where will you learn more tangible skills? Which projects will look better on your resume?

- **The Company & Culture:** Where did you feel a better 'vibe' during the interviews? Which company's mission are you more passionate about?

- **The Future Potential:** Which company has a stronger track record of hiring its interns for full-time roles? Which brand name will open more doors for you in the long run?

Once you've made your decision, you need to communicate it professionally to both companies. Accept the one you want with an enthusiastic phone call and written confirmation. For the one you're declining, be gracious and appreciative.

- **The 'Gracious Decline' Script:** "Dear [Recruiter Name], Thank you again so much for the generous offer to join your team this summer. It was a difficult decision, but I have decided to accept another position that aligns more closely with my long-term career goals at this time. I was so impressed by your team and the work you're doing, and I would love to stay in touch for future opportunities."

THE ETHICS OF RENEGING: A WORD OF CAUTION

Reneging, accepting an offer and then backing out later for a different one, is a tricky and controversial topic. Let me be direct: in the corporate recruiting world, this is a big deal. When you accept an offer, the company stops recruiting for that role. They take down the posting, they tell the other candidates 'no,' and they start the onboarding process. When you back out, you send them scrambling and can burn a bridge not just for yourself, but sometimes for your university's reputation with that company.

While there can be extreme circumstances, my strongest advice is to avoid reneging if at all possible. Use the strategies above to ask for an extension so you can make your final decision *before* you say 'yes.' Your professional reputation is your most valuable asset, and it starts being built now.

⚙ ACTIVITY: YOUR HIGH-STAKES SCRIPT BUILDER

STEP ONE: THE 'I NEED MORE TIME' SCRIPT:

Imagine you received an offer from your second-choice company with a three-day deadline, but you know you have a final interview with your top choice next week. Write out the exact script you would use in an email to ask for an extension.

STEP TWO: THE 'GRACIOUS DECLINE' SCRIPT:

You've decided to accept an offer from Company A. Write out the exact email you would send to the recruiter at Company B to decline their offer professionally and keep the relationship positive.

THE BOTTOM LINE

How you handle the final stages of your internship search is a direct reflection of your professionalism. By communicating clearly, acting with integrity, and making thoughtful, holistic decisions, you're not just choosing an internship. You're building the foundation of a strong professional reputation that will serve you for your entire career.

GETTING GHOSTED & OTHER BUMMERS: HOW TO HANDLE REJECTION

Let's talk about the job search's worst parts. The endless inbox refreshing, waiting for a reply that never comes. The polite, generic rejection email after hours spent on an application. The complete ghosting after what felt like a great interview. This part? It just sucks, no matter where you are in your career.

For students who are used to excelling academically, where hard work usually leads to a good grade, this part of the process can feel brutal and deeply personal. It's natural to feel frustrated, disappointed, or even question if you're good enough.

So, let me pull back the curtain from my side of the hiring desk and tell you something with absolute certainty: rejection is a normal, expected, and fundamental part of the job search. It happens to everyone. The secret isn't learning how to avoid it; it's learning how to handle it like a pro.

THE REALITY OF CORPORATE RECRUITING: IT'S NOT ALWAYS ABOUT YOU

It's crucial to understand why you might face rejection, because most of the time, it has absolutely nothing to do with your qualifications or potential.

- **The Sheer Volume:** Large companies receive thousands of applications for a handful of spots. It's a mathematical reality that even hundreds of highly qualified candidates will be rejected.

- **The 'Fit' Puzzle:** Sometimes a team isn't just looking for a skill; they're looking for a specific personality to balance out their group, or someone with a niche experience that wasn't even in the job description. It's not a judgment of you; it's about their specific, immediate need.

- **The Power of Referrals:** As we've discussed, an internal referral is a massive advantage. Sometimes, a role is unofficially filled by a referral before the external process even gets going.

- **The Shifting Business:** Corporate priorities change in an instant. I've seen entire internship programs get scaled back or canceled due to budget cuts long after applications have opened.

- **The Robot Gatekeeper:** Even a minor formatting glitch can cause the ATS to filter out a perfect resume before a human ever sees it. It's a technical hurdle, not a reflection of your capability.

- **The Rolling Clock:** Many companies hire on a rolling basis. Applying late in the cycle, even if you're a perfect candidate, can mean you're out of the running simply because all the spots have already been filled.

YOUR PLAYBOOK FOR BOUNCING BACK

Instead of viewing rejection as a personal failing, think of each 'no' as a data point, a practice run for the 'yes' you're truly meant to get. Here's how to shift your mindset and leverage rejection to your advantage.

- **Acknowledge the Sting (Briefly):** It's okay to be bummed out. Give yourself an hour to be frustrated. Go for a walk. Listen to music. Vent to a friend. But then, you have to move on. Dwelling on it is what allows self-doubt to creep in and kill your motivation.

- **Don't Take it Personally:** Say it out loud: "This was a business decision, not a personal one." Your skills, intelligence, and potential are still 100% valid.

- **Seek Feedback (When Appropriate):** If you made it to an interview, it's okay to politely ask for feedback. Send a simple, professional email: "Thank you again for the opportunity. While I understand the decision, I'm always looking to grow. If you have a moment, I'd be grateful for any constructive feedback that could help me improve for future opportunities." Be prepared to not get a response (some recruiters are better than others with this), but when you do, it's gold.

- **Analyze and Iterate:** This isn't about beating yourself up; it's about refining your strategy. Did you tailor your resume enough? Were your STAR stories as strong as they could be? Use what you learn to make your next application even better.

- **Celebrate the Small Wins:** Did you get a phone screen? That's a win! It means your resume worked. Did you make it to a final round? That's a huge win! It means you're a top-tier candidate. Acknowledge these successes to maintain your confidence.

BUILDING RESILIENCE: THE LONG-TERM GAME

Resilience isn't just about surviving tough times; it's the critical skill that separates successful professionals from everyone else. Every 'no' you face now is a chance to build this muscle.

- **Diversify Your Search (Beyond the Obvious):** Don't put all your hopes on one or two famous companies. Apply to a diverse range of organizations: large corporations, mid-sized companies, startups, and non-profits. Find adjacent companies that might provide services to your 'famous' target. Broadening your scope not only increases your odds but also exposes you to amazing opportunities you might have otherwise missed.

- **Continuously Develop Your Skills:** Use a rejection as fuel. Did a technical interview expose a weak spot? Dedicate time to practicing. Did you struggle to articulate your contributions? Work on your STAR stories. The internship search is a feedback loop: what you learn from a 'no' should directly inform where you build your skills next.

- **Focus on What you can Control:** You can't control how many people apply for a job or if a company has a last-minute budget change. Dwelling on those things will burn you out. Instead, pour your energy into what you *can* control: the quality of your resume, your interview preparation, your networking efforts, and your positive attitude.

💡 INSIDER INSIGHT: THE 'NO' THAT LED TO A 'YES'

I once worked with an exceptionally talented student who was initially rejected from our summer internship program. Naturally, he was disappointed, but instead of giving up, he sent a thoughtful thank-you note and asked to stay in touch. Over the next six months, he focused on a personal project that directly addressed a technical challenge he knew our company was working on. When a last-minute internship opening came up in that same department the following spring, I immediately thought of him. His initiative and proactive follow up stood out. That first 'no' wasn't the end; it became the catalyst for a more strategic and ultimately successful 'yes.'

⚙️ ACTIVITY: YOUR RESILIENCE GAME PLAN

Managing rejection is about building the emotional muscle to bounce back stronger. Let's build your personal game plan.

STEP ONE: LEARNING FROM A PAST SETBACK

- Think of a time you faced a rejection or disappointment (academic, extracurricular, etc.).

- **Initial Reaction:** How did you react at first?

- **Key Lesson Learned:** What is the most important lesson you took away from that experience that you can apply to your internship search?

STEP TWO: PRE-EMPTING FUTURE DISAPPOINTMENT

- It's empowering to understand why rejections happen.

- **Beyond Your Control:** List two to three common reasons for rejection that are truly beyond your control. When you get a 'no,' remind yourself of these.

- **Within Your Control:** List two to three reasons for rejection that *are* within your control. For each, note one specific, actionable step you'll take to improve.

- **Example:** Reason: Weak STAR stories in interviews | Action: Practice two to three STAR stories aloud with a peer before my next interview.

STEP THREE: YOUR RESILIENCE STATEMENT

- Create a short, powerful personal statement (one to two sentences) that you can revisit when you feel discouraged. This statement should reaffirm your value and your commitment to your goals.

- **Example:** "Rejection is redirection. Every 'no' brings me closer to the right 'yes,' and I will continue to learn and grow."

By actively engaging in this reflection, you're not just reacting to setbacks; you're proactively building the mental fortitude and strategic approach needed to succeed.

THE BOTTOM LINE

Let's call rejection what it is: a workout for your resilience muscle. And right now, you're in training. The first time you get a 'no,' it's going to leave you sore for days. It hurts. The tenth time? It still stings, but you recover faster. The fiftieth time? You barely break your stride.

This isn't about getting numb; it's about getting stronger. Every rejection proves you're in the game, you're taking chances, and you're trying. It is not a sign of failure. It is evidence of effort. Don't let a 'no' from a company you won't even remember in five years derail the career you're going to have for the next 40. Grieve it for an evening, then wake up tomorrow and get back to your workout. The right 'yes' is worth all the 'no's' it takes to get there.

DECODING YOUR DREAM: EVALUATING AND NEGOTIATING YOUR INTERNSHIP OFFER

You see it in your inbox. The subject line says, "Internship Offer from [Company Name]." Your heart starts pounding. You open it, you read the word 'Congratulations,' and for a moment, you feel like you've reached the finish line. You did it. All the research, the resume drafts, and the interview prep paid off. You should absolutely take a moment to celebrate this huge win.

But this isn't the finish line. It's the start of a new level of the game. What you do in the next few days can shape your entire summer experience and even your future career. The temptation is to immediately hit 'Accept!' without a second thought. Don't. Pause. Take a breath. It's time to put your detective hat back on and approach this strategically. This is your opportunity to ensure the internship aligns perfectly with your goals.

UNDERSTANDING THE OFFER: IT'S MORE THAN JUST THE MONEY

An internship offer is a complete package, not just a single hourly figure. It's crucial to look beyond the pay and carefully consider all the components.

Thinking holistically about the offer will help you make the best decision for your unique situation. Let's break down the key components you need to evaluate:

COMPENSATION:

- **Hourly Wage / Stipend:** Is the rate competitive for your industry, role, and location? Use resources like your university's career services, Salary.com, and Glassdoor to find out.

- **Overtime Pay:** Are you eligible? How is it calculated?

- **For Unpaid Internships:** Will you get academic credit? Is there significant, structured mentorship? Will you work on real projects that build your resume? Be very critical here.

DURATION AND SCHEDULE:

- **Start and End Dates:** Do these align with your academic calendar?

- **Hours per Week:** Is it a full-time or part-time position? Is there flexibility for classes or exams?

THE ROLE ITSELF (THE MOST IMPORTANT PART):

- **The Work:** What will you *actually* be doing? Ask for specific examples of projects past interns have worked on if you had not done so during the interview process.

- **Learning Opportunities:** Will you get exposure to new technologies or training?

- **Mentorship:** Will you have a dedicated mentor? How often will you meet with your manager?

LOGISTICS & PERKS:

- **Location:** Is it in-person, remote, or hybrid?

- **Housing / Relocation:** Is any support offered if you need to move?

- **Conversion Potential:** Does the company have a strong track record of hiring its interns for full-time roles? This is a huge indicator of how much they invest in their program.

THE ART OF NEGOTIATION: ASKING FOR WHAT YOU DESERVE

Many students are terrified of negotiating. You think, "I don't want to appear greedy," or "What if they pull the offer?" Let me tell you an insider secret: a respectful, well-prepared negotiation shows confidence and professionalism. Most companies *expect* you to negotiate a little, even for internships. It's a positive signal that you're engaged and serious about the opportunity.

WHEN TO NEGOTIATE: THE GOLDEN RULES

- **After a firm offer is extended:** Never negotiate before you have an official offer in writing.

- **Before you accept:** Once you say 'yes,' your negotiating power is gone. You typically have a few days to a week to consider an offer, so use that time wisely.

WHAT YOU CAN NEGOTIATE (IT'S NOT JUST ABOUT SALARY):

- **Hourly Wage / Stipend:** This is the most common, but not the only, point of negotiation.

- **Start / End Dates:** Companies are often flexible by a week or two if you have a legitimate academic conflict.

- **A Relocation Stipend:** If you're moving to a high-cost-of-living city, it's reasonable to ask for a small stipend to help with moving costs.

- **A Specific Project:** "I'm really passionate about your work in [X area]. Would there be an opportunity for me to contribute to a project related to that?"

HOW TO NEGOTIATE (STEP-BY-STEP)

Negotiating is a conversation, not a confrontation. Approach it with confidence and professionalism.

1. **Express Enthusiasm and Gratitude:** Always begin by thanking them sincerely for the offer and reiterating your excitement. "Thank you so much for the offer! I'm genuinely excited about the chance to contribute to the team."

2. **Gather Your Justification (Your 'why'):** Don't just ask for more. Clearly and concisely explain *why* your request is reasonable.

   o **Competing Offer:** "I've also received an offer from another company at $X per hour. I'm much more excited about your opportunity, and I was wondering if there's any flexibility on the compensation?"

o **Market Research:** "Based on my research for similar roles in this industry and location, the typical hourly rate seems to be in the range of [slightly higher figure]. Given this, I was hoping we could discuss the compensation."

3. **Make a Specific Request:** Be clear, concise, and direct. "Would you be able to increase the hourly rate to $X?" or "Would it be possible to offer a small relocation stipend to help offset the initial expenses?"

4. **Listen Actively:** After making your request, pause and listen carefully to their response.

5. **Get it in Writing:** Any agreed-upon changes should always be confirmed in a revised written offer letter.

☀ INSIDER INSIGHT

The Negotiation That Sealed the Deal: I once extended an offer to a student who came back with a thoughtful question. She said, "I'm incredibly excited about this offer. My only concern is that I'll be moving from out of state. Would it be possible to offer a small stipend to help with the security deposit on a temporary apartment?" It was a reasonable, well-justified request that we hadn't considered. We were able to approve a small stipend, and her professional, confident approach made us even more excited to have her join the team.

⚙ ACTIVITY: YOUR OFFER DECONSTRUCTION & NEGOTIATION GAME PLAN

STEP ONE: THE OFFER LETTER AUTOPSY

Use the sample offer letter below. Identify and annotate the key components. What's clear? What's missing? What two questions would you ask the recruiter to get more clarity?

Sample Offer Letter:

Dear [Student Name],

On behalf of ACME Inc., we are pleased to extend to you an offer for the position of Marketing Analytics Intern. This is a paid, temporary internship based at our headquarters in Nashville, Tennessee.

Position Title: Marketing Analytics Intern

Reporting Manager: Jill Higgins, Marketing Manager

Start Date: Tuesday, September 2, 2025

End Date: Friday, December 12, 2025

Work Schedule: Approx. 20 hours per week, flexible schedule.

Compensation: $18 per hour

Contingencies: This offer is contingent upon a background check.

We are incredibly excited about the prospect of you joining our team.

Sincerely,

The ACME Inc. Recruiting Team

STEP TWO: PRACTICE YOUR NEGOTIATION SCRIPT

Let's role-play. You've received the offer above, but your research shows the average rate for this role in Nashville is closer to $20 / hour. Draft a short, professional script for your conversation with the recruiter.

_____

_____

_____

_____

_____

_____

_____

_____

_____

_____

_____

- **Express enthusiasm:**

- **Justify your wage request (based on market research):**

- **State your specific wage request:**

- **Conclude gracefully:**

THE BOTTOM LINE

You've got an offer in your inbox. Feels like you just hit the lottery, right? Don't be that kid who takes the first shiny object just because it's handed to them. This isn't the finish line; it's the *starting line* for your professional career. By evaluating it thoughtfully and being prepared to negotiate respectfully, you're not being difficult; you're being a professional. You're taking the first step in actively managing your career, a skill that will serve you long after this internship is over.

HOW TO NOT BE BROKE DURING YOUR INTERNSHIP

Internships are amazing for your career, your resume, and your future 'adulting' skills. But here's the cold, hard truth: unless you're independently wealthy or living off parental generosity, you'll need to figure out how to pay for this 'internship' thing.

This chapter isn't about getting rich, but it is about understanding the money game when it comes to internships. We're going to break down the financial realities and give you some battle-tested strategies to manage your cash like a pro, so you can focus on crushing your internship, not stressing about your bank account.

SHOW ME THE MONEY: A GUIDE TO GETTING PAID

Internships come in all flavors, and some are tastier than others when it comes to your wallet. You need to know the menu before you order.

PAID INTERNSHIPS: THE GOLD STANDARD (MOSTLY)

- **Hourly Wages:** This is what most students are looking for. You work; you get paid. Simple. The rate is all over the map, so do your homework. Use sites like Glassdoor, Payscale, and your university's career center to know the going rate for your role and location.

- **Stipends: the Fixed-Rate Deal.** Sometimes, you get a set amount for the whole internship. To figure out if it's a good deal, do the math: divide the total stipend by the total hours you expect to work. Is that hourly rate worth your time?

- **Tax Implications: Uncle Sam Wants his cut.** Here's the buzzkill: anything you earn is generally taxable. Don't be surprised when your paycheck is less than you thought. Plan for it.

UNPAID INTERNSHIPS: THE 'BENEFITS MUST BE HUGE' OPTION

- **The Legal Lowdown (FLSA): Don't Get Exploited.** Listen up: in the U.S., unpaid internships have strict rules. They have to benefit *you* more than the employer (think academic credit, serious training). If it smells like free labor, it probably is.

- **Is it Worth it? Ask the Tough Questions.** If an internship is unpaid, the 'compensation' comes in other forms. You must weigh these benefits like they're gold. Ask yourself:

  - **Academic Credit?** Can this count toward your degree?

  - **Exceptional Learning?** Are you going to learn something genuinely rare and valuable?

  - **Networking Nirvana?** Will you be rubbing shoulders with people who can open doors for you later?

- o **Portfolio Power-Up?** Will you walk away with actual work samples that make future employers say, "WOW!"?

- **The Reality Check: Can you Actually Afford it?** This is the hardest part. Don't take an unpaid internship if it means you'll be drowning in debt, failing classes because you're working a second job just to pay rent, or living on air. This is the time to have a frank and open conversation with your support system. If your parents or family are assisting with your tuition, this is a conversation you need to have with them. Be prepared to discuss your budget and how this unpaid experience is a strategic investment in your future. Also, talk to your financial aid office or a trusted mentor. Sometimes, a lower-paying *paid* internship is better than a 'free' one that breaks you.

OTHER COMPENSATION: THE HIDDEN PERKS

Companies sometimes offer benefits beyond the paycheck that can save you serious cash. Always ask about:

- **Housing Help:** A stipend or corporate housing can be a game-changer in a pricey city.

- **Transportation Tidbits:** Public transit passes or parking reimbursement add up.

- **Food & Fun:** Free meals, company events, and gym memberships can seriously cut down your expenses.

💡 INSIDER INSIGHT: THE LAST-MINUTE BACK-OUT

Nothing created more of a fire drill for my recruiting team than when an intern would accept an offer, only to back out two weeks before the start date because they 'couldn't make the finances work.' It would leave the hiring manager in a tough spot and, frankly, it reflected poorly on the student's planning skills.

On the flip side, I remember a candidate who, upon receiving an offer for an internship in a very expensive city, came back to us with a polite and professional question. They said, "I am incredibly excited about this opportunity. To make my final decision, could you connect me with a former intern who participated in the program? I'd love to ask them a few questions about budgeting for housing in the area."

That student wasn't just asking for money; they were demonstrating incredible maturity and foresight. They were treating their finances as a serious part of their professional planning. We were not only happy to connect the past and future interns, but it also made us even more confident that we had chosen a responsible and proactive future employee. Your financial preparedness is a reflection of your overall professionalism.

BUDGETING FOR YOUR INTERNSHIP: DON'T BE A FINANCIAL TRAIN WRECK

Whether you're raking in the big bucks or just getting by, a solid budget is your superhero cape against financial stress.

- **Estimate EVERYTHING:** Before you start, map out every single expense: Housing, Transportation, Food, Personal Stuff, and an 'Oh Crap Fund' for emergencies.

- **Track it Like a Hawk:** Use a simple spreadsheet or a budgeting app like Mint or YNAB. This isn't about judging yourself; it's about seeing where your money actually goes so you can adjust.

- **Find Ways to Pinch Pennies:** This isn't about being cheap; it's about being smart.

  o **Roomies Rule:** Sharing rent is almost always cheaper.

  o **Cook, Don't buy:** Packing lunches will save you a fortune.

  o **Free fun is the Best fun:** Explore parks, free museum days, and community events.

  o **Flash That Student ID!** Always ask for student discounts.

FINANCIAL AID AND INTERNSHIPS: THE MONEY YOU MIGHT LOSE (OR KEEP!)

Okay, this is important. Most students act like their financial aid office is some kind of a secret society, but these people are there to help you. And trust me, you *need* to talk to them, especially if you snag a paid internship, because that extra cash might mess with your current or future financial aid.

- **Talk to Your Financial Aid Office (ASAP!):** Make an appointment before you accept a paid offer. They know your specific aid package and can give you the real talk.

- **Income Reporting:** Internship income needs to be reported on forms like FAFSA and can affect your financial aid in future years. Know this upfront.

- **Scholarships & Grants:** Some scholarships have rules about outside income. Read the fine print so you don't accidentally violate the terms.

💡 INSIDER INSIGHT: DON'T BE NAIVE ABOUT FINANCES

I once coached a brilliant student who landed a high-paying tech internship. He was so excited, he immediately signed a lease on a fancy apartment. What he didn't do was talk to his financial aid office. The next year, his need-based grants were significantly reduced because of his summer income, and he was left scrambling to cover tuition. It was a stressful, avoidable mistake. A single 30-minute meeting with his adviser could have saved him months of anxiety.

THE LONG-TERM VALUE: YOUR FUTURE SELF WILL THANK YOU

Even if your internship is unpaid, or barely pays enough to cover gas money, don't miss the forest for the trees. This experience is a massive, long-term investment in your future earning potential.

- **Accelerated Skill Development:** You'll learn more practical skills in a few months on the job than you might in a full year of lectures.

- **Powerful Networking:** The people you meet are your future network. They can lead you to your next, better-paying job.

- **Enhanced Resume Building:** A solid, relevant internship instantly boosts your resume and often leads to better salary offers for your first full-time gig.

- **Clearer Career Trajectory:** Companies often hire their interns full-time after they graduate. This means a smoother transition, often at a higher salary, than if you were applying cold.

⚙ ACTIVITY: YOUR 'NO EXCUSES' FINANCIAL GAME PLAN

STEP ONE: RESEARCH AVERAGE SALARIES:

- Pick a target internship role. Now go find out what it pays in a specific city. Use Glassdoor, Payscale, and your university's career center. Know your worth.

STEP TWO: CREATE A SAMPLE BUDGET:

- Choose a city where your dream internship might be. Map out all your monthly expenses for a 10-12 week internship. Be realistic. This is where you see if your dream is affordable.

STEP THREE: CONTACT YOUR FINANCIAL AID OFFICE:

- This is non-negotiable. Make a plan to email or meet with your financial aid adviser. List two specific questions you will ask.

STEP FOUR: LIST THREE WAYS TO SAVE MONEY:

- Brainstorm three specific, actionable ways *you* could cut costs and save money during an internship.

THE BOTTOM LINE

Don't be naive about internship finances. Be proactive. Understand your compensation, how it impacts your financial aid, and how to budget like a boss. The financial literacy you gain now will serve you well for life.

THE WAITING GAME: WHAT TO DO BEFORE DAY ONE

You did it. Offer signed. Summer set. Congratulations! For a moment, the hard part feels over. But now comes a weird, new phase: the waiting game.

It might be months before your first day, and that time isn't just dead air. It's a crucial period to maintain momentum and set yourself up for a great first impression. The work you do now ensures you walk in on day one feeling prepared and confident, not stressed and scrambling. Let's break down how to master this 'pre-game' period.

HOW TO STAY ON THEIR RADAR (WITHOUT BEING ANNOYING)

Many large companies will stay in touch with their incoming intern class. This isn't just them being nice; they're continuing to build a connection and, frankly, making sure you're still excited and engaged. From a recruiter's perspective, we're not just checking a box; we're investing in you and want to ensure a smooth transition.

- **Be Hyper-Responsive:** If a recruiter sends an email with updates or a welcome webinar invitation, respond promptly. A quick "Thanks so much for the update, looking forward to it!" shows you're engaged and professional. For us, a quick response means you're organized and eager, which bodes well for your future contributions.

- **Keep Your Grades up:** Don't get senioritis. Many offers are contingent on you staying in good academic standing. A sudden drop in your GPA can be a red flag. Finish the semester strong to show you're a person who follows through. Remember, your academic performance reflects your ability to manage responsibilities and deliver results—qualities we look for in every hire.

- **Handle Your Paperwork Immediately:** You will get emails about background checks, drug tests, and other HR paperwork. Do not procrastinate on this. Respond immediately and complete all the required steps. Any delay on your part can delay your start date or create a headache for the recruiting team. This isn't just bureaucracy; it's essential for getting you onboarded efficiently. Your promptness here directly impacts your ability to start on time and hit the ground running.

YOUR PRE-FIRST DAY CHECKLIST: HOW TO NOT LOOK LIKE A ROOKIE

Being prepared is the best cure for first-day jitters. This isn't about studying; it's about handling the simple logistics so you can focus on what matters.

THE WEEK BEFORE:

- **Confirm the Logistics:** Reread your offer letter or welcome email. Double-check the exact start date, time, and address. For remote roles, confirm the time zone. Know the name of the person you're supposed to ask for when you arrive.

- **Do a Final Recon Mission:** Re-familiarize yourself with the company. What have they been in the news for since you interviewed? Look up your manager and a few potential teammates on LinkedIn again. Knowing their faces and roles makes introductions less awkward.

- **Plan Your Commute (Seriously):** If you're working in person, do a test run of your commute during rush hour. Figure out the traffic, the parking, or the train schedule. Have a backup plan. Nothing is more stressful than being late on your first day.

- **The Dress Code:** If you're unsure what to wear, it is always okay to ask your recruiter. A simple, "What's the typical dress code for the office?" is a smart question. When in doubt, it's always better to be slightly overdressed.

- **Bring Necessary Documentation:** Every U.S. company will require documentation for your I-9 form and W-2. Make sure you have your proper IDs in hand.

💡 INSIDER INSIGHT: THE FORGETFUL INTERN

I once saw an incredibly promising intern lose their dream opportunity on day one, not due to lack of skill, but due to a simple oversight. Despite multiple reminders, they arrived without the necessary I-9 documentation (like a passport or driver's license and Social Security card). When they couldn't produce the required forms within the strict three-day federal deadline, the company, due to compliance regulations, had no choice but to terminate their internship. It was a heartbreaking situation, a stark reminder that even the smallest administrative detail can have major professional consequences. Always prioritize your HR paperwork!

THE NIGHT BEFORE:

- **Lay out Your Outfit:** Don't leave this until morning. Have your entire professional outfit ready to go.

- **Pack Your bag:** Get your notebook, pens, laptop, chargers, water bottle, and any required ID documents (like a passport or driver's license for I-9 verification) packed and by the door.

- **Set two Alarms:** Trust me on this.

WHAT TO EXPECT ON YOUR FIRST DAY: A WHIRLWIND OF "HI, MY NAME IS ... "

Your first day is going to be an information overload. Don't expect to be handed a massive, world-changing project at 9:05 a.m. Your main job is to listen, learn, and be a sponge.

- **The Paperwork Parade:** Expect to spend a good chunk of time on HR onboarding—tax forms, direct deposit, and signing agreements.

- **The IT Adventure:** A big part of your day will be getting your tech set up: your laptop, your passwords, and your access to different systems. This can sometimes take hours. Be patient. Bring a notebook to review any company materials they've given you while you wait.

- **The Introduction Tour:** You'll meet your manager, your team, and probably a bunch of other people whose names you will immediately forget. That's okay. Focus on being friendly, making eye contact, and remembering the names of the people on your direct team.

- **The Information Overload:** You'll be hit with a firehose of new acronyms, project names, and team structures. You are not expected to remember everything. Your job is to take great notes and ask smart questions.

💡 INSIDER INSIGHT: THE MOST IMPRESSIVE FIRST-DAY QUESTION

The interns who impressed me most on day one weren't the ones who acted like they knew everything. They were the ones who showed they were eager to learn the right way. After their manager gave them an overview, they'd ask a simple but powerful question: "What's the best way for me to ask questions when I get stuck? Should I come to you directly, ask a teammate, or use our team's chat channel?" This question shows incredible self-awareness and respect for your team's workflow. It tells your manager you're a proactive, considerate professional from the very beginning.

⚙️ ACTIVITY: YOUR FIRST DAY GAME PLAN

Imagine your first day at your dream internship is next Monday.

STEP ONE: YOUR 'NIGHT BEFORE' CHECKLIST:

- What are three specific, non-negotiable things you will do the night before to prepare?

STEP TWO: YOUR 'SMART QUESTIONS' LIST:

- What are three thoughtful questions you will have ready for your manager or team on day one?

STEP THREE: YOUR FIRST-WEEK MINDSET:

- What is one positive mindset goal you will set for yourself for the first week? (e.g., "My goal is to learn the name of every person on my direct team," or "I will focus on listening more than I speak in meetings.")

THE BOTTOM LINE

Your internship doesn't start on your first day; it starts the moment you accept the offer. By being professional, proactive, and prepared during the waiting period, you set the stage for a successful summer. You're showing your new team that they made the right choice in hiring you before you even step foot in the office.

THINGS YOU'LL WISH YOU KNEW ON DAY ONE

Your internship is underway! The first few weeks? A blur of new names, new projects, and the quest for good snacks. Beyond the actual work your manager assigns you, you have three other incredibly important jobs during this time: being a detective, a great communicator, and the most reliable person in the room.

Mastering these 'unwritten rules' of the workplace will make a bigger impact on your success than you can imagine. This chapter is your guide to navigating the professional environment like a pro from day one.

YOUR FIRST JOB: BE A WORLD-CLASS OBSERVER

Every company has its own unique personality, or 'culture.' It's the collection of unspoken rules, norms, and communication styles that dictate how things *really* get done. Your primary mission in the first two weeks is to observe and adapt.

- **Decode the Dress Code:** Is it full-on business casual with slacks and button-downs, or are nice jeans and sneakers the norm? Observe what your team and manager are wearing and aim to match that level of professionalism. When in doubt during your first week, it's always better to be slightly overdressed. You can always dress down later.

- **Figure out the Communication Flow:** Is everything done through formal, detailed emails, or is the team's Slack or Microsoft Teams channel where the real work happens? Pay attention to how people ask questions, give updates, and share information. Do people respond to messages instantly, or is a several-hour delay normal? Matching the communication style is a key part of fitting in.

- **Read the Room in Meetings:** Are meetings a rapid-fire brainstorm where everyone jumps in, or is there a more structured, formal process where you wait to be called upon? In virtual meetings, are cameras usually on or off? Is it common for people to interrupt with questions? Your job is to match the energy and etiquette of the room. In your first few meetings, your main job is to listen and learn.

- **Understand the Work-Life Vibe:** Do people consistently work late and send emails at all hours, or is there a strong emphasis on leaving on time and disconnecting? Notice when your manager and teammates log off for the day. This gives you a clue about the team's expectations around work-life balance.

YOUR SECOND JOB: BE AN EXCELLENT COMMUNICATOR

In the professional world, *how* you say something is just as important as *what* you say. Clear, concise, and professional communication builds trust and prevents misunderstandings.

- **Over-Communicate Your Progress:** Especially in the beginning, your manager will appreciate knowing what you're working on. They are busy, and a quick update saves them from having to chase you down. A simple end-of-day email or Slack message like, "Just a quick update: I finished the research for Project X and will start analyzing the data tomorrow," is a simple way to show you're on top of things.

- **Ask for Clarification Immediately:** If you're unsure about an assignment, ask for clarification *before* you start working. A simple, "Just to make sure I'm on the right track, the main goal here is X, correct?" can save you hours of wasted effort. It shows you're thoughtful, not incompetent.

- **Be Prompt and Professional:** Respond to emails and messages in a timely manner. Even a quick "Got it, I'll get back to you on this by the end of the day" shows you're responsive and manages expectations.

YOUR THIRD JOB: BE INCREDIBLY RELIABLE

Trust is the currency of the professional world, and the fastest way to build it is by being reliable. This is the single most important trait you can demonstrate.

- **Be Punctual:** Arrive on time (or a few minutes early) for work and all meetings, whether they're in-person or virtual. Lateness signals disrespect for other people's time.

- **Meet Your Deadlines:** Consistently deliver your work when you say you will. This is the bedrock of a professional reputation.

- **Communicate Proactively About Delays:** If you see a potential roadblock or think you might miss a deadline, communicate it to your manager as early as possible. Don't wait until the last minute. Explain the reason and propose a revised timeline. This shows maturity and respect for the team's workflow.

💡 INSIDER INSIGHT: DON'T BE THAT INTERN

I once had an intern who, on paper, was perfect. But they consistently missed deadlines, showed up late to meetings, and the work they submitted was subpar. We provided coaching and feedback, but the behavior didn't change. Despite the intern's initial qualifications, lack of professionalism and reliability made the decision not to extend a full-time offer an easy one. Remember, your internship is a long job interview. How you show up every day makes a huge difference.

DECODING THE SECRET LANGUAGE: ACRONYMS & JARGON

Every company has its own language of acronyms and jargon. You'll be hit with a firehose of new terms on day one. Don't panic. No one expects you to know what 'TPS reports' or 'Q3 KPIs' are right away.

- **Keep a Running List:** Start a 'New Acronyms' list in your notebook or a digital document. This will become your personal glossary. When you hear a new term, jot it down. Pro tip: some organizations keep a glossary of company-specific jargon and acronyms. Ask for it and bookmark it, early.

- **Use Context Clues:** Listen actively in meetings. Often, you can figure out the meaning of a term from the conversation around it.

- **Ask Smartly:** If you're genuinely stuck, it's okay to ask a trusted colleague or your manager. Wait for a good moment (not in the middle of a high-pressure presentation) and frame it smartly. A simple, "I'm still learning the lingo here, could you clarify what 'EOD' means?" shows you're engaged and eager to learn.

- **Note:** a complete list of acronyms can be found in the Appendix.

⚙ ACTIVITY: YOUR FIRST-WEEK SURVIVAL KIT

STEP ONE: CULTURE OBSERVATION CHALLENGE:

- For your first week, make it a point to observe your workplace culture.

  o Identify one example of informal communication (e.g., how people chat in Slack).

  o Identify one example of formal communication (e.g., the tone of a company-wide email).

  o Identify one 'unwritten rule' you've noticed (e.g., "Don't schedule meetings on Friday afternoons" or "Everyone eats lunch at their desk").

STEP TWO: ACRONYM DECODER:

- Start your 'New Acronyms' list. Your goal is to capture at least five new terms in your first week and find out what they mean.

STEP THREE: RELIABILITY CHECK-IN:

- At the end of your first week, ask yourself: Was I on time for every meeting? Did I meet every small deadline? Did I communicate my progress clearly?

INSIDER INSIGHT: BE CURIOUS AND CORAGEOUS

One of my favorite work days of the year is the day we kick off our Summer Internship Programs. The energy of the interns and their excitement to learn can be felt throughout the company. During the onboarding sessions the interns that stand out are the ones that aren't afraid to take a risk and speak up, raise their hands to ask or answer a question, or try something new. Be one of the interns who actively participates in the sessions and keep that curiosity going through the summer.

Remember that your internship is one long continuous interview; you want to start off strong and also maintain your momentum through the summer.

THE BOTTOM LINE

The first few weeks of your internship are less about proving you know everything and more about proving you're a curious, reliable, and professional person to have on the team. By focusing on observing the culture, communicating clearly, and being incredibly dependable, you'll build a strong foundation of trust that will set you up for a successful and impactful summer.

CORNERSTONES OF COMMUNICATION: HOW TO NOT SOUND LIKE A ROOKIE

Your actual work might be brilliant, but if your communication makes you sound like you're still in a dorm room, it'll hold you back. Every email you send, every Slack message you type, and every comment you make in a meeting, that's not just talking; it's your personal brand in action. It's how you build your professional reputation. It's how you prove you're a credible, reliable, and thoughtful colleague.

In the last chapter, we talked about observing the 'unwritten rules' of the office. This chapter is your tactical guide to mastering them. We're going to break down the art of business communication, from crafting the perfect email that actually gets read, to knowing exactly when a GIF is a genius move and when it's an absolute, career-limiting disaster. Let's make sure your words elevate you, not undermine you.

THE SIX SIGNALS YOU'RE SENDING WITH EVERY MESSAGE

Whether you're speaking or writing, you're always sending signals. Internalize these six principles, and you'll always make a strong impression.

- **Clarity Signals Respect:** Being direct and unambiguous shows you respect the other person's time. State your main point early and avoid jargon they might not know.

- **Conciseness Signals Intelligence:** Getting to the point efficiently, without unnecessary words, shows you can think clearly.

- **Professionalism Signals Maturity:** Maintaining a respectful tone and using appropriate language shows you understand the context of the workplace.

- **Audience Awareness Signals Empathy:** Tailoring your message and knowing how to talk to your manager versus a peer versus a senior executive shows you understand other people's perspectives.

- **Active Listening Signals Collaboration:** Listening to understand, not just to wait for your turn to talk, is the foundation of all great teamwork.

- **Timeliness Signals Reliability:** Responding promptly shows you are on top of your work and dependable.

MASTERING PROFESSIONAL EMAIL: YOUR DIGITAL HANDSHAKE

Email is the official record of the business world. It's your digital handshake and a lasting impression. Getting it right is a non-negotiable skill.

ANATOMY OF A PERFECT PROFESSIONAL EMAIL

Let's break down a strong email, piece by piece.

> **Subject:** FEEDBACK REQUEST for Project Z Draft by EOD Friday
>
> Dear Alex,
>
> I hope you're having a productive week.
>
> I'm writing to request your feedback on the first draft of the Project Z marketing slides, which I have attached to this email.
>
> Could you please review the attached presentation and provide any comments or suggestions by the end of the day this Friday, July 26th? Your insights on the competitive analysis slides (five to seven) would be particularly helpful.
>
> Thank you in advance for your time and feedback.
>
> Best regards,
>
> [Your Name]
>
> Summer Intern, Marketing
>
> [Company Name]

Let's break down why this works:

- **The Subject Line: Your First Impression**

  o It's clear, specific, and tells the recipient exactly what's needed and by when.

  o **Weak:** 'Update'

  o **Best:** 'FEEDBACK REQUEST: For Project Z Draft by EOD Friday'

- **The Salutation: Setting the Tone**

  o When in doubt, be more formal. Use "Dear Mr. / Ms. / Mx. [Last Name]" for new contacts or senior leaders. "Hi [First Name]" is perfect for colleagues you know.

- **The Body: Clear, Concise, and Action-Oriented**

  o The first sentence states the purpose. The body provides context and makes a clear 'ask' with a bolded deadline. The paragraphs are short and easy to scan.

- **The Closing & Signature**

  o Use a professional closing like 'Best regards' or 'Sincerely.' Always include your full name, title, and company.

💡**INSIDER INSIGHT: THE EMAIL THAT MADE ME SAY 'NO'**

I once had an intern who was brilliant in person but terrible at email. Their messages were long, rambling streams of consciousness with no clear point. One time, they sent me a three-paragraph email that was really just asking for a simple deadline. It took me five minutes to figure out what they needed. It signaled to me that they couldn't organize their thoughts and didn't respect my time. That seemingly small issue was a major factor in our decision not to extend a full-time offer. Your emails are a reflection of your thinking. Make them clean and clear.

BEYOND EMAIL: CHOOSING THE RIGHT COMMUNICATION TOOL

The modern workplace runs on multiple platforms. Using the right one shows you understand efficiency and respect your colleagues' workflow.

INSTANT MESSAGING (SLACK, MICROSOFT TEAMS)

- **Best for:** Quick questions, fast updates, informal check-ins, and sharing links.

- **Key Etiquette:** Get to the point. Avoid sending 'Hi' and then waiting. Type your full question in one message. Respect the 'Do Not Disturb' status.

VIRTUAL MEETINGS (ZOOM, GOOGLE MEET)

- **Best for:** Team syncs, project discussions, presentations, and any conversation that benefits from screen sharing or seeing faces.

- **Key Etiquette:** Mute by default. Mind your background. Follow your team's norm on cameras (but having it on usually shows more engagement).

PHONE CALLS

- **Best for:** Urgent or sensitive topics, or resolving complex issues that are getting confusing over email.

- **Key Etiquette:** Always start by asking, "Is now a good time to talk for a few minutes?"

⚙ ACTIVITY: PRACTICE YOUR POLISH

STEP ONE: EMAIL REDRAFT CHALLENGE

Read the 'Weak Example' email below. Then, using the principles from this chapter, rewrite it into a 'Strong Example.'

- **Weak Example:**

  Subject: quick q
  Hey [Manager's Name],

  Just wanted to ask about that thing with Project Z. Like, when is it due? I kinda forgot and don't want to mess up.

  Thx!
  [Your First Name]

- **Your Strong Example Draft:**

_____

_____

_____

STEP TWO: CHANNEL CHOICE CHALLENGE

For each scenario below, which communication channel would you choose (Email, IM, Virtual Meeting, or Phone Call) and why?

- **Scenario:** You discovered a major error in a data report that is scheduled to be presented to a client by your manager in one hour.

- **Your Choice & why:**

_____

_____

_____

- **Scenario:** You want to ask your teammate if they have a link to the company's holiday schedule.

- **Your Choice & why:**

_____

_____

_____

- **Scenario:** You need to get formal approval from your manager for a new software subscription that costs $50 / month. You need to include the link to the software and the justification for it.

- **Your Choice & why:**

_____

_____

_____

THE BOTTOM LINE

The principles in this chapter may seem like a long list of details, but they are the building blocks of your professional identity. Mastering them isn't just about following rules; it's about being strategic. The care you put into your messages builds a foundation of trust. The clarity you provide earns you respect. In the modern workplace, this isn't a 'soft skill'; it is a power skill, one that ensures your great work is seen, understood, and valued.

HOW TO NOT BE ANNOYING: A GUIDE TO THE UNWRITTEN RULES OF THE OFFICE

Beyond your technical skills and project contributions, your ability to navigate the unspoken rules of the workplace or 'office etiquette' significantly impacts your success and reputation. Good etiquette demonstrates respect, professionalism, and an understanding of the shared environment. It's about being a considerate colleague and a valued team member.

THE FOUNDATION: RESPECT AND AWARENESS

At its core, office etiquette is about respect for your colleagues, the shared space, and the company's time and resources.

- **Observe and Adapt:** Your primary tool for learning etiquette is observation. Watch how senior colleagues behave, communicate, and interact. Different companies and teams will have slightly different norms.

- **Empathy:** Think about how your actions affect others. Is your noise distracting? Is your mess impacting someone else?

- **Professionalism First:** When in doubt, err on the side of more formal and professional behavior, especially early in your internship.

KEY AREAS OF OFFICE ETIQUETTE

PERSONAL SPACE AND NOISE LEVELS:

- **Respect Boundaries:** Be mindful of personal space at desks, in common areas, and during conversations. Avoid leaning over someone's shoulder or touching their belongings without permission. While you might be curious, what's on a person's screen is private unless otherwise shared with you directly.

- **Manage Noise:**

  - **Phone Calls:** Take personal calls outside the immediate work area, or keep them very quiet and brief. Use headphones for virtual meetings or calls if in an open office.

  - **Headphones:** Fine for focusing, but remove them when someone approaches you to indicate you're available for interaction.

  - **Conversations:** Keep your voice level appropriate for the environment. In open offices, lower your voice.

SHARED SPACES: KITCHENS, BREAK ROOMS, AND RESTROOMS:

- **Cleanliness is Crucial:** Always clean up after yourself.

  - **Kitchen:** Wash your dishes immediately or put them in the dishwasher. Wipe up spills. Don't leave food to spoil in the fridge. Label your food if that's the norm.

  - **Microwave:** Cover your food to prevent splatters. Wipe any spills.

o **Common Areas:** Leave meeting rooms tidy. Push in chairs.

MEETINGS: IN-PERSON AND VIRTUAL:

- **Punctuality:** Arrive on time (or a few minutes early) for all meetings. Lateness is disrespectful of others' time.

- **Be Prepared:** Bring what you need (notebook, pen, and laptop). Review the agenda if provided.

- **Active Participation:**

  o Listen Actively: Give your full attention. Multitasking is more obvious than you think.

  o Contribute Thoughtfully: If you have something valuable to add, speak up. Don't dominate the conversation.

  o Take Notes: Essential for remembering action items and key decisions. Embedded note-taking tools in platforms like Slack and MS Teams can help keep you organized.

- **Technology use in Meetings:**

  o **Phones:** Put your phone on silent / vibrate and avoid checking it during meetings.

  o **Laptops:** Use your laptop only for meeting-related tasks. Avoid browsing the internet or doing other work.

    o **Virtual Meetings:** In hybrid office setups, many colleagues may dial in remotely. Be mindful and inclusive of their attendance and give them room to participate.

DRESS CODE:

- **Observe First:** If not explicitly stated, observe what others in similar roles or your team wear.

- **Err on the Side of Professionalism:** It's always better to be slightly overdressed than underdressed, especially during your first week.

GENERAL OFFICE DEMEANOR:

- **Be Approachable:** Smile, make eye contact, and be open to interaction.

- **Positive Attitude:** Maintain a positive and enthusiastic demeanor. Avoid complaining or excessive negativity.

- **Respect Everyone:** Treat all colleagues, regardless of their role or seniority, with respect.

- **Confidentiality:** Interns may have access to sensitive information. Never discuss confidential company matters outside the office.

- **Network Gracefully:** Don't constantly interrupt people for networking. Respect their work time.

- **Say 'Please' and 'Thank You':** Basic manners go a long way.

- **Don't Gossip:** Steer clear of office politics and gossip. It's unprofessional and can quickly damage your reputation.

- **Take Initiative (Appropriately):** While being proactive is good, don't overstep your bounds or take on tasks without discussing them with your manager first.

💡 INSIDER INSIGHT: THE 'DEATH BY A THOUSAND PAPER CUTS' INTERN

I remember an intern who was technically brilliant, but their daily habits drove the team crazy. They'd take loud personal calls at their desk, leave their lunch mess in the kitchen for hours, and constantly interrupt senior colleagues in meetings. Individually, these were small things. But added up over a summer, they created a reputation that this person was inconsiderate and lacked professional awareness. When it came time to discuss full-time offers, even though their project work was good, the team just couldn't see themselves working with that person long-term. Your daily etiquette isn't just about being polite; it's about proving you're a considerate colleague people want to have around.

⚙ ACTIVITY: ETIQUETTE SCENARIO PLANNING

For each scenario, describe the best etiquette-driven response:

- **Scenario One:** You spilled coffee on the break room counter near the sink.

- **Your Action:**

_____

_____

_____

- **Scenario Two:** You overhear two colleagues in the cubicle next to you discussing a confidential company project loudly.

- **Your Action:**

_____

_____

_____

- **Scenario Three:** You need to ask a quick question of a colleague who is wearing headphones at their desk.

- **Your Action:**

_____

_____

_____

- **Scenario Four:** You arrive five minutes late to a virtual team meeting because your internet briefly went out.

- **Your Action:**

_____

_____

_____

THE BOTTOM LINE

Your technical skills might get your foot in the door, but your office etiquette? That's what decides if they actually want you to stay. This isn't about being a robot; it's about being a pro. Every little thing, from cleaning your coffee mess to keeping your voice down, builds your reputation, or slowly, painfully, destroys it. You want to be the intern they fight to keep, the one people actually want to work with? Then understand the unwritten rules and prove you're not just smart, but also a decent human being. That's how you go from being an intern to being a colleague who makes the team better.

YOU'RE IN! HOW TO BE THE INTERN THEY CAN'T LIVE WITHOUT

You did it. You navigated the applications, aced the interviews, and landed the offer. Take a moment to celebrate; you've earned it.

Now, the real game begins.

Your internship is not just a summer job; it's a 10- to 12-week-long interview for a full-time position. Every project, every meeting, and every interaction is an opportunity to prove that you are not just a capable student, but an indispensable future colleague. Companies invest in internship programs with the primary goal of finding their next generation of talent. Your mission is to make their decision easy. This chapter is your playbook for turning a great opportunity in to a career-launching success.

THE FIRST PROJECT: YOUR MOMENT TO SHINE

Sometime in your first week, your manager will give you your first significant project. This is a test. They're not just evaluating the final product; they're evaluating your process, your resourcefulness, and your attitude.

- **Deconstruct the ask.** Don't just nod and run back to your desk. Before you start, make sure you understand the assignment completely.

  o **Ask Clarifying Questions:** "Just to make sure I'm on the right track, the primary goal of this analysis is X, correct?" "What does a successful outcome look like for this project?" "Is there a specific format you'd like for the final report?"

  o **Confirm the Deadline:** "To confirm, the deadline for this is next Friday at 5 p.m.?"

- **Create a Mini-Plan.** Take 30 minutes to break the project down into smaller, manageable steps. This shows you're a strategic thinker, not just a task-doer.

- **Provide a Mid-Point Check-in.** Don't disappear for a week and then reappear with the finished product. About halfway to the deadline, send your manager a brief, proactive update.

  o **Example:** "Hi [Manager's Name], just a quick update on the competitor analysis project. I've completed the initial research on Companies A and B and plan to analyze C and D by tomorrow. So far, the insights are pointing towards X. I'm on track to have the full draft to you by our Friday deadline."

- **Deliver Early (if Possible).** Aim to finish your project a day before the deadline. This gives you time to do a final proofread and gives your manager time to review it without being rushed.

ASKING FOR MORE WORK (THE RIGHT WAY)

At some point, you might finish a task and find yourself with downtime. Your instinct might be to sit quietly and wait for your next assignment. Don't. Proactively seeking work shows initiative, but there's an art to doing it without being annoying.

- **The Wrong Way:** "I'm bored. Do you have anything for me to do?" (This makes you sound like a burden.)

- **The Right Way:** "I just finished the data entry for the X project. I have some extra bandwidth this afternoon—is there a smaller task I could help with to support the team's goals?" (This is professional, specific, and team-oriented.)

- **The Pro-Level Move:** Before you even ask your manager, ask a teammate. "Hey, I have a few free hours. Is there anything I can take off your plate to help you prepare for the big presentation?" This shows you're a true team player.

THE MID-POINT CHECK-IN: YOUR PERFORMANCE REVIEW PREVIEW

About halfway through your internship, you should proactively ask your manager for a mid-point check-in. This is your chance to get formal feedback, course-correct if needed, and make sure you're on track to hit your goals.

- **How to Ask:** "Hi [Manager's Name], as we're now at the halfway point of my internship, I was hoping we could schedule 20 minutes to chat about my progress. I'd love to get your feedback on how I'm doing and discuss what I can focus on for the second half to make the biggest impact."

- **Key Questions to Ask During the Meeting:**
  - o "From your perspective, what is one thing I'm doing well that I should continue?"
  - o "What is one area where I could improve or a skill I should focus on developing?"
  - o "Am I on track to meet the goals we set for this internship?"
  - o "How can I best support you and the team in the final few weeks?"

💡 INSIDER INSIGHT: THE INTERN WHO ASKED FOR FEEDBACK

I once managed an intern who was good, but not great. He was quiet and did his work, but he wasn't making a huge impression. Halfway through the summer, he scheduled a meeting with me and asked those exact questions. His proactive request for feedback completely changed my perception of him. It showed me he was self-aware, driven, and serious about his growth. We had a great conversation, he implemented the feedback immediately, and he ended up being one of the top interns we hired that year. Don't wait for feedback; go get it.

THE FINAL PRESENTATION: YOUR CLOSING ARGUMENT

Many internships culminate in a final presentation where you share your project and your learnings with the team or even senior leaders. This is your final opportunity to shine.

- **Focus on Impact, Not Just Activity:** Don't just list what you *did*. Frame your presentation around the *results* of your work.

  o **Instead of:** "First, I gathered data. Then, I put it in a spreadsheet..."

  o **Try:** "My project goal was to understand X. By analyzing Y, I discovered Z, which could potentially help the team save 10% on costs."

- **Know Your Audience:** Are you presenting to your direct team or to senior executives? Tailor your message. Your team might want the technical details; executives want the high-level summary and the 'so what?'

- **Practice, Practice, Practice:** Rehearse your presentation out loud multiple times. Time yourself. Anticipate questions and prepare answers.

- **End with Gratitude:** End your presentation by genuinely thanking your manager, your mentor, and your team for the opportunity and their guidance.

⚙ ACTIVITY: YOUR INTERNSHIP GAME PLAN

You don't have to wait until your first day to be strategic.

STEP ONE: YOUR FIRST PROJECT 'PRE-MORTEM':

- Think about the type of role you're targeting. What is one potential 'first project' you might be given? What are two clarifying questions you would ask your manager before you start?

STEP TWO: YOUR 'DOWNTIME' SCRIPT:

- Write out the exact sentence you will use when you have downtime and want to ask for more work.

STEP THREE: YOUR MID-POINT CHECK-IN REQUEST:

- Draft the email you will send to your future manager to request a mid-point review.

THE BOTTOM LINE

A successful internship isn't about being perfect; it's about being professional, proactive, and passionate about learning. By tackling your projects with a strategic mindset, actively seeking feedback, and communicating your value effectively, you're not just completing an internship. You're making an undeniable case for why you belong on the team for the long haul.

HOW TO GET YOUR BOSS TO LOVE YOU (A GUIDE TO 1:1S)

It pops up on your calendar: '1:1 with [Manager's Name].' Your first thought? A mix of 'Cool!' and 'Oh crap, what do I talk about for 30 minutes?' The temptation is to walk in, wait for your manager to ask questions, and when they say, "So, how are things going?" you give the classic, safe answer: "Good!"

This is a massive wasted opportunity. Your 1 : 1 (one-on-one) meetings with your manager are arguably the most important regular touchpoints of your internship. These aren't just status updates; they are dedicated time slots for your growth, feedback, and career guidance. Learning to prepare for and lead these meetings is the fastest way to build trust and prove your value.

THE POWER OF 1:1S: YOUR INTERNSHIP'S SECRET WEAPON

Don't just clock in; lean into those one-on-one (1:1) meetings. These aren't your typical check-ins; they're your opportunity to take control of your internship. This is *your* turf, where you seize the moment, ask the smart questions, get the lowdown before small stuff blows up, and lay out exactly what you need to crush it.

Want more on your plate? Wrestling with a tough assignment and need a lifeline? Got an innovative idea that could make the team shine? The 1:1 is your moment to make things happen. Walk in with a game plan: solid questions, your non-negotiables, and an open mind, even for the tough truths. That's how you turn a routine meeting into your personal launchpad.

PREPARING FOR YOUR 1:1: DON'T WALK IN BLIND – MASTER THE ART OF PRE-MEETING STRATEGY

A great 1:1 doesn't just happen; it's engineered. Success starts long before you even step in the room. This isn't just about getting ahead; it's about showing respect for your manager's packed schedule and proving you're in the driver's seat of your own career.

- **Review Previous Notes: The Foundation of Continuity** Before you show up, hit rewind. What went down last time? Any assignments for you, or for them? And the big one: did you act on that feedback? Showing you're on top of things proves you're in it to win it.

- **Summarize Your Progress: Quantify Your Impact** Be ready to brag, but keep it tight. Think 'Accomplishment + Quantifiable Result' (A+Q). Ditch the vague "I worked on the survey" and go for: "I dissected the recent customer survey data. Boom! Feature X's user engagement shot up 15%, thanks to those UI tweaks. That's a win." Show them the numbers, show them the impact.

- **Come with an Agenda: Your Roadmap for a Purposeful Discussion**
  This is your secret weapon. Don't sit there like a bump on a log waiting for the manager to lead. You walk in with your own blueprint, your own list of what needs to be discussed. This ensures your biggest concerns and your growth targets are front and center, making every minute count.

DURING THE 1:1: MAKING THE MOST OF THE TIME – EXECUTE WITH PRECISION AND PURPOSE

This meeting is your stage. Every second is a chance to learn, get clear, and push your agenda.

- **Be Punctual: Respecting Shared Time**

  Show up on time, every time. It's not just polite; it's a statement. You respect their time, and you mean business.

- **Drive the Conversation: Seize the Initiative**

  Take the wheel. Start strong: "Thanks for making time. I've got a few key items I want to hit to make sure we maximize this," or "Appreciate this dedicated time. Unless you've got a fire to put out, I've teed up some specifics that tie directly into my progress and growth." You set the tone, you control the narrative.

- **Be Honest and Transparent: Embrace Challenges as Learning Opportunities**

Don't bury the tough stuff. Hiding problems just creates bigger headaches down the road. Lay it out, but frame it as a hurdle you're tackling, not a dead end.

- **Instead of:** "This project's killing me." (Weak. Vague. Unhelpful.)

- **Try:** "I'm elbow-deep in Project X and hit a wall. I've already thrown Solutions A and B at it, but the technical snag on C is still there. Your two cents on this would be huge, or maybe you could point me to the right resource" (Smart. Proactive. Asking for a specific assist.)

- **Take Detailed Notes: Documenting Progress and Commitments**
Scribble everything down. Action items, decisions, feedback – it's all gold. This isn't just for memory; it's your battle plan, ensuring everyone's on the same page and nothing slips through the cracks.

- **Clarify Action Items: Cementing Accountability**
Before you wrap, lock it down. "So, just to be clear, my mission is to scope out X's feasibility by Friday's stand-up, and you're linking me with the Y team for their API insights, right?" No room for misinterpretation. Everyone knows their marching orders.

💡 INSIDER INSIGHT: THE INTERN WHO TALKED HIMSELF INTO A JOB

I once managed two interns on the same team. Both were smart and did good work. But one of them, 'Mark,' truly mastered the 1:1. Every week, he came in with a clear agenda: "Here's what I finished, here's where I'm stuck, and here are two ideas for the next phase of the project." The other intern would just say, "Everything's going fine." Guess who got the bigger, more interesting projects? Mark did. He used his 1:1s to prove he wasn't just a task-doer; he was a strategic thinker. When it came time to extend a full-time offer and we only had one spot, the decision was easy. Mark had used his 1:1s to make himself appear indispensable.

AFTER THE 1:1: THE FOLLOW-THROUGH: MAXIMIZING IMPACT BEYOND THE MEETING

Your work isn't done when the meeting ends; in fact, the real opportunity to solidify your professional reputation and demonstrate your initiative often begins *after* the 1:1. The actions you take in the hours and days following a meeting can significantly amplify the value of the discussion and showcase your commitment to growth and excellence. Think of it as a quiet but powerful ripple effect.

- **Review Your Notes: The Immediate Synthesis.**

  Immediately after the meeting, dedicate a short, focused block of time to review and clean up your notes. This isn't just about legibility; it's about clarity and actionability. Expand on shorthand, clarify any ambiguous points, and most importantly, highlight key decisions, action items, and feedback points. Organize them logically, perhaps by topic or by priority. This immediate synthesis ensures you don't lose crucial details and transforms raw notes into a valuable, organized record that will guide your subsequent actions. Consider what you need to remember, what you need to do, and what you learned. It's like distilling the essence of the conversation.

- **Execute on Your Follow-Ups: Building the Bedrock of Trust.**

  This is perhaps the most critical step. Do *exactly* what you said you were going to do, and do it promptly. If you promised to send a report, send it. If you committed to researching a particular topic, begin that research immediately. If you offered to help a colleague, reach out. Consistently executing on your follow-ups builds trust with your manager and colleagues. It demonstrates reliability, accountability, and a strong work ethic. It shows that you value their time and that your word is your bond. Over time, this consistency establishes you as a dependable and valuable member of the team. Think of it as laying your foundation brick by brick.

- **Implement Feedback: The Path to Accelerated Growth.**

  Nothing makes a manager happier than seeing an intern who actively listens and demonstrates a genuine desire to grow. Make a conscious, visible effort to apply the advice and feedback you received during

266

the 1:1. If your manager suggested a different approach to a task, try it. If they recommended a resource for skill development, explore it. If they pointed out an area for improvement in your communication, focus on refining it in your next interactions. Don't just acknowledge feedback; *act* on it. If possible, circle back with your manager to show them how you've implemented their suggestions, demonstrating your commitment to continuous improvement and your appreciation for their guidance. It's a subtle but powerful way to show you're serious.

COMMON 1:1 PITFALLS TO AVOID: NAVIGATING PRODUCTIVE CONVERSATIONS

While 1:1s are invaluable, they can also become unproductive if not approached thoughtfully. Avoiding these common pitfalls will ensure you maximize the benefits of these dedicated discussions.

- **The 'I Have Nothing to Discuss' Trap: A Major Missed Opportunity**

  Walking into a 1:1 without a prepared agenda or with the dismissive phrase, "I have nothing to discuss," is a major missed opportunity. It signals a lack of initiative, engagement, and foresight. Your 1:1 is your dedicated time with your manager – a chance to get clarity, receive guidance, address challenges, and discuss your development. Always come prepared with updates on your progress, specific questions about your work or career trajectory, and topics for discussion. This demonstrates you are actively thinking about your role and contributing to your own success. Don't let this precious time slip away.

- **Using it as a Complaint Session: Frame Concerns Constructively.**

While 1:1s are a safe space to raise concerns or challenges, they should not devolve into a mere complaint session. Constantly airing grievances without proposing solutions or reflecting on your role in the situation can be draining and unproductive. If you have a concern, frame it constructively. Describe the problem objectively, explain its impact, and then propose potential solutions or ask for your manager's guidance on how to move forward. Focus on collaboration and problem-solving rather than just airing frustrations. It's about solutions, not just problems.

- **Only Talking About Problems: Balance Challenges with Accomplishments.**

It's easy to focus on what's difficult or what isn't working, but a productive 1:1 requires balance. While discussing challenges is essential for getting support, it's equally important to highlight your accomplishments, progress, and what's going well. Share what you've learned, what you've successfully completed, and how you've contributed. This provides a holistic view of your performance, showcases your contributions, and allows your manager to see your growth and positive impact. Show the full picture.

- **Not Taking Notes: A Sign of Disengagement and a Recipe for Forgetfulness.**

Failing to take notes during a 1:1 is a significant misstep. You will inevitably forget details, action items, and crucial feedback. More importantly, it can give the impression that you are not fully engaged or that you don't value the discussion. Taking notes shows active listening, respect for your manager's time and insights, and a commitment to remembering and acting on what was discussed. Even if you think you'll remember, jotting down key points ensures accuracy and provides a valuable reference for your follow-through. It's a subtle but important cue of professionalism.

⚙ ACTIVITY: YOUR NEXT 1:1 AGENDA BUILDER: PROACTIVE PREPARATION FOR SUCCESS

Imagine you have a 1:1 scheduled with your manager next week. Proactively building an agenda ensures you make the most of this valuable time and demonstrates your preparedness and initiative. Fill out the following agenda template, tailoring it to your current work and developmental goals:

STEP ONE: UPDATES & ACCOMPLISHMENTS (SINCE LAST 1:1):

This section is your opportunity to highlight your progress and value. Be specific and quantify your impact whenever possible. *(List two to three key accomplishments, e.g., "Completed initial research for Project X, providing a comprehensive competitive analysis report," "Finalized Z report and sent to client ahead of deadline, receiving positive feedback on data visualization." Quantify impact if possible, e.g., "Reduced manual data entry time by 15% on Task A," or "Contributed to a 5% increase in engagement on social media campaign B.")*

STEP TWO: CURRENT CHALLENGES / ROADBLOCKS & SUPPORT NEEDED:

This is where you seek guidance and remove obstacles to your productivity. Be clear about the challenge and precise about the help you need. *(Describe one to two challenges, e.g., "I'm struggling with understanding the advanced functions of Y software, particularly the data aggregation feature; could you recommend a tutorial or provide a brief overview?" "I need access to the Z database to complete my analysis for the upcoming presentation; could you facilitate that access or advise on the correct procedure?" Specifically state what help you need.)*

STEP THREE: QUESTIONS / DISCUSSION TOPICS:

Use this section to drive your learning, career development, and clarify future steps. These should be open-ended questions that encourage discussion. *(List two to three specific questions, e.g., "What are the next steps for Project A, and what is the expected timeline for its completion?" "How can I improve my communication and presentation skills in team meetings, particularly when presenting complex data?" "Are there any opportunities to learn more about the X department's operations, or perhaps shadow someone in that area to broaden my understanding of the company?")*

THE BOTTOM LINE

Your 1:1s? They're not just check-ins; they're your personal coaching sessions. By showing up prepared, owning the conversation, and following through, you're not just being a good intern – you're proving you're a future leader. This isn't about ticking a box; it's about building a relationship, showing you're invested, and making sure you get what you need to turn this internship into something far bigger. Stop treating 1:1s like detention and start treating them like your personal strategy sessions. That's how you make these connections truly count.

WHAT TO DO WHEN YOUR BOSS IS A DUD (AND HOW TO SAVE YOUR OWN INTERNSHIP)

You pictured it, right? Your internship manager: a mentor / guide / cool professor meets savvy industry pro. They'd offer challenging projects, insightful feedback, and a clear path through the corporate world.

But instead, you got a dud.

Maybe your boss is a ghost who you only see in passing. Maybe they're so overwhelmed with their own work that they forgot you exist. Or maybe the only 'project' they've given you is organizing a decade-old supply closet. It's one of the most disheartening experiences an intern can have. You feel stuck, invisible, and like you're wasting your summer.

Let's be clear: it's a crummy situation, but it is not a dead end. In fact, learning how to succeed without a great manager is one of the most valuable 'real-world' skills you can develop. This chapter will show you how to save your own internship and turn this challenge into a story of incredible initiative.

FIRST, DIAGNOSE YOUR DUD

Not all dud bosses are created equal. Identifying the type you're dealing with is the first step to creating a strategy.

- **The Ghost:** This manager is never around. They're always traveling, in 'important' meetings, or working from home. You barely see them, and getting a response to an email takes days.

- **The Delegator of Drudgery:** This manager sees you as a pair of hands, not a brain. Your tasks consist of the boring, administrative work no one else wants to do: making copies, formatting spreadsheets, or other mind-numbing assignments.

- **The Overwhelmed One:** This manager isn't a bad person; they're just drowning in their own work. They had great intentions for your internship, but a massive project just landed on their desk, and managing you has fallen to the bottom of their 100-item to-do list.

YOUR PROACTIVE PLAYBOOK: HOW TO MANAGE UP

Your manager isn't defining your internship experience; *you* are. Here's how to take control.

STRATEGY FOR 'THE GHOST': BECOME THE ULTIMATE COMMUNICATOR

If your boss isn't present, you have to create that presence for them.

- **Master the Proactive Update Email:** At the end of every week, send your manager a concise, bulleted email.

  Subject: Weekly Internship Update - [Your Name]

  Hi [Manager's Name],

  Just a quick summary of my week:

  - Completed the analysis of the Q2 sales data.

  - Created a first draft of the presentation deck for the marketing team.

  - Met with Sarah from the product team to learn about the upcoming launch.

  My focus for next week is to finalize the presentation deck. Please let me know if you have any feedback.

  Best,

  [Your Name]

- **Find a Proxy Mentor:** Identify another helpful, experienced person on your team. It could be a senior analyst or a project manager. Ask them for guidance. They can often provide the day-to-day feedback your ghost manager can't.

STRATEGY FOR 'THE DELEGATOR OF DRUDGERY': THE 'YES, AND ... ' METHOD

The key here is to crush the crap work with a great attitude, and then leverage that to get more.

- **Crush the Boring Work:** Do the mindless tasks faster and better than anyone expects. Become the most reliable person in the office for getting things done. This builds trust.

- **Use the 'Yes, and ... ' Technique:** When they give you a boring task, say 'Yes,' and then ask for more. "Absolutely, I can get those slides formatted for you. And since I'll be finished with that this afternoon, I was wondering if I could also help the team with the market research for the new project I heard about in yesterday's meeting?"

- **Create Your Own Project:** Did you notice an inefficient spreadsheet or an outdated process? Spend a few hours creating a better version. Then, present it to your boss: "I had some downtime and noticed X, so I created a potential solution. Could I walk you through it for 10 minutes?"

STRATEGY FOR 'THE OVERWHELMED ONE': MAKE THEIR LIFE EASIER

This manager needs an intern who reduces their stress, not adds to it.

- **Batch Your Questions:** Don't ping them with a new question every 20 minutes. Keep a running list and ask for a quick 15-minute sync-up once a day to go through them all at once.

- **Bring Solutions, Not Just Problems:** When you get stuck, try to solve it yourself first. When you do go to them, frame it like this: "I'm running into an issue with X. I've already tried A and B. My next thought is to try C, but I wanted to get your advice first."

💡 INSIDER INSIGHT: THE INTERN WHO SAVED HERSELF

We once had an intern whose manager was unexpectedly pulled into a one-month-long corporate crisis and became a total ghost. The intern could have sat at her desk and done nothing. Instead, she befriended a senior analyst on the team who taught her our internal data systems. She noticed the team was tracking project statuses on a messy spreadsheet, so she used her downtime to build a simple but brilliant automated dashboard to track everything. By the time her manager resurfaced, the intern wasn't just 'keeping busy'; she had become a critical part of the team's workflow. She didn't just save her own internship; she proved she was a leader. We hired her, and she got promoted twice in three years.

WHEN TO ESCALATE: THE 'BREAK GLASS IN CASE OF EMERGENCY' OPTION

Sometimes, despite your best efforts, the situation is unsalvageable or unhealthy. If your manager is truly preventing you from having any meaningful experience, or if the issue is more serious (unethical behavior, harassment), you may need to escalate it.

Your first point of contact should be the overall internship program manager, human resources, or your university recruiter contact. Approach them professionally. Don't complain; present the situation calmly and focus on your desire to learn.

"Hi [Recruiter Name], I'm really enjoying my time here. I'm running into a small challenge with my project assignments and was hoping to get your advice on how I can make sure I'm contributing and learning as much as possible this summer."

This gives them the context they need to step in and help, whether it's by talking to your manager or finding you a supplemental project.

THE BOTTOM LINE

A 'dud boss' can feel like a disaster, but it's actually an opportunity in disguise. It's a chance to prove that you are a resilient, proactive, and resourceful problem solver, the very qualities every company wants to hire. Your manager doesn't define your internship experience. You do.

PART V:
THE INTERNSHIP IS OVER...
BUT THE GAME IS JUST BEGINNING

How to turn a great summer experience into a powerful career asset for the long haul.

THE INTERNSHIP IS OVER. NOW WHAT?

It's your last day. Laptop returned, goodbyes said, and you walk out for the final time. A weird mix of relief (no more 7 a.m. alarms!), sadness, and a big, looming question: 'Now what?'

Congratulations! You survived and hopefully thrived. You gained real-world experience, made some connections, and learned a lot. But the end of an internship isn't the finish line; it's the beginning of your next strategic move. The work you do in the next few weeks is what turns a great summer experience into a powerful career asset.

Your employer likely will send you a survey to see how your experience was. Take the time to respond and provide honest feedback. The Campus Recruiting teams put a lot of work into making your summer special and want to continually improve for the next cohort of interns. This chapter is your guide to making it all count.

MAKING THE MOST OF YOUR EXPERIENCE: CONDUCT A PERSONAL DEBRIEF

Before you dive back into classes and forget all the details, you need to conduct a personal debrief. Your memory of the projects, challenges, and accomplishments is sharpest right now. Don't let it fade. Grab a notebook and spend an hour answering these questions. This isn't just journaling; it's mining for the gold you'll use in your resume and future interviews.

WHAT DID YOU ACTUALLY LEARN?

- **Skills:** What new technical skills did I pick up? Be specific: name the software (e.g., Salesforce, Adobe Premiere, Figma), the programming language (e.g., Python, JavaScript), or the analytical tool (e.g., Google Analytics, advanced Excel functions).

- **Soft Skills:** What professional skills did I practice? Think about specific moments. Did you present to a team of 10 people? Did you manage a project with a two-week deadline? Did you collaborate with another department to solve a problem?

- **Industry Knowledge:** What do I understand now about this industry that I didn't before? What are the big challenges or trends? For example, "I learned that in the consumer goods industry, supply chain logistics are the biggest factor impacting product launch timelines."

- **Self-Discovery:** What tasks gave me energy, and what tasks drained me? Did I love the fast-paced, collaborative brainstorming sessions but dread the detail-oriented data entry? Did this experience confirm my interest in this career path, or did it make me want to run in the opposite direction? (Both are valuable discoveries!)

WHAT DID I ACTUALLY ACCOMPLISH?

- **Projects:** What were the two or three main projects I worked on? What was my specific role and what was the ultimate outcome?

- **Contributions:** How did my work help the team or the company? Did I solve a nagging problem, improve a clunky process, or create something from scratch?

- **Quantify Everything:** Now is the time to attach numbers and metrics to your work.

  o **Before:** "Helped with the social media accounts."

  o **After:** "Developed and scheduled content for three social media platforms, resulting in a 15% increase in follower engagement over two months."

  o **Before:** "Organized some files."

  o **After:** "Reorganized the team's shared digital drive, creating a new file-naming system that reduced the time needed to find documents by an estimated 25%."

- Think in terms of **time saved, money saved, percentage increased,** or the **number of people** your work impacted.

LEVERAGING YOUR NETWORK: DON'T BECOME A GHOST

The connections you made during your internship are your most valuable takeaway. Don't let them fizzle out. Nurturing these relationships is a professional skill.

- **Send a Thank-You Note:** Within a week of leaving, send a personalized thank-you email to your manager, your mentor, and a few key colleagues who helped you. Mention a specific thing you learned from them and express your gratitude for their guidance.

- **Connect on LinkedIn (The Right Way):** Send a connection request to everyone you worked with. Don't use the generic template. Try something like "Hi [Name], it was such a pleasure working with you on the [Project Name] team this summer. I'd love to stay in touch!"

- **Ask for Recommendations and References (Now!):** The best time to ask for a LinkedIn recommendation or for someone to be a future reference is while you're still fresh in their mind.

  o Example: "Hi [Manager's Name], I really valued your guidance this summer. If you feel comfortable doing so, would you be willing to write a brief LinkedIn recommendation for me based on my work on [Project Name]? I'd also be grateful to know if I could list you as a reference for future opportunities."

💡 INSIDER INSIGHT: WHAT HAPPENS AFTER YOU LEAVE

Here's a secret: after the interns leave, the managers, HR teams, and recruiters all get together to talk about them. We literally go down the list, person by person, and ask the big question: 'Would we bring them back next summer or hire them full-time?' The interns who performed well and brought their best self every day were always top of mind. The interns who stayed connected, sent thoughtful thank-you notes, and asked for recommendations were the ones we thought of first. They made it easy for us to remember their impact and advocate for them when full-time roles opened up. Don't disappear.

POST-INTERNSHIP PLANNING: CHARTING YOUR NEXT COURSE

With your reflections and networking in mind, it's time to plan your next moves.

UPDATE YOUR RESUME AND LINKEDIN (IMMEDIATELY):

- **Add Your Internship Experience:** While the details are fresh, add your new experience to your resume and LinkedIn. Use the powerful A+Q bullet points you just brainstormed.

- **Highlight New Skills:** Add all the new technical and soft skills you gained to your skills sections.

REFINE YOUR JOB SEARCH STRATEGY:

- **Target Companies and Roles:** Based on your internship, do you want more of the same, or something different? Did you discover that you prefer a small, fast-paced team over a large corporate structure? Use these insights to refine your 'hit list' of companies.

SET NEW GOALS:

- **Short-Term:** What's your immediate goal for the upcoming semester? This could be landing another internship for the spring, taking a specific class to fill a skill gap you discovered (like public speaking or a coding class), or getting a leadership position in a campus club to practice your management skills.

- **Long-Term:** How did this internship affect your long-term career goals? Did it solidify your plan or inspire a new direction?

⚙️ ACTIVITY: YOUR POST-INTERNSHIP ACTION PLAN

STEP ONE: LIST THREE KEY LEARNINGS:

- Identify three significant things you learned during your internship about yourself, the industry, or a specific skill.

STEP TWO: QUANTIFY TWO ACCOMPLISHMENTS:

- Choose two accomplishments from your internship and write them out as powerful, quantified bullet points for your resume.

STEP THREE: IDENTIFY TWO CONTACTS TO RECONNECT WITH:

- Name two individuals from your internship network you will send a personalized thank-you note and LinkedIn request to this week.

STEP FOUR: SET ONE SHORT-TERM CAREER GOAL:

- Define one achievable career goal for the next three to six months, based on your internship experience.

THE BOTTOM LINE

The post-internship period is a crucial time for consolidating your learning, expanding your professional network, and planning your future. By taking the time to reflect, connect, and strategize, you can maximize the value of your internship and set yourself up for future success.

THE GAME IS JUST BEGINNING

You've reached the end. The work is done, from defining your path to decoding the corporate recruiting machine and acing the interview. If you've followed the plays, you're no longer an outsider. You have the insider's perspective.

The goal of this book was to pull back the curtain and show you how large companies *really* think, operate, and hire, cutting through the noise and bad advice from 'gurus' who have never sat on my side of the hiring desk. Now, when you face the internship search, you're not just guessing; you're operating with a proven strategy.

As you move forward, keep the core of the book with you. These are the non-negotiables:

- **Know Your 'Why'** A successful search starts with knowing what you truly want and what matters to you. This clarity is the foundation for everything else and will be your compass when you have to make tough decisions.

- **Be a Detective, Not a Spammer** Ten highly tailored, well-researched applications will always beat 200 generic, copy-pasted ones. Do your research, show you care, and prove you're interested in *their* company, not just *any* company.

- **Tell a Story of Impact** Your resume is a marketing document, not a history report. Every bullet point is a chance to sell your value. Use powerful action verbs and hard numbers to prove your impact and make them *see* your potential.

- **Network with Purpose** Your goal is not to collect contacts; it's to build genuine relationships that lead to advice, advocacy, and opportunity. A warm referral from a trusted employee is worth more than a thousand online applications.

- **Embrace Rejection as Redirection** You will get 'no's. Every successful person does. The key is to learn from them, build your resilience, and never take it personally. It's a business decision, not a judgment of your worth.

- **Act Like a Professional, Always** Punctuality, preparation, clear communication, and a positive, can-do attitude are what separate the good interns from the ones who get full-time offers.

Remember, landing the internship isn't the finish line. It's the starting line for the rest of your professional life. Your career is a marathon, not a sprint, and the skills you've just practiced: resilience, strategic thinking, professional communication, and networking are the very skills that will help you succeed for decades to come.

You are now equipped with the insider knowledge and the practical tools to not only land an internship but to thrive in it. You have the playbook. Go out there with confidence, with curiosity, and with the determination to build a career that is not only successful but also uniquely and authentically yours.

Your journey is just beginning.

MY FINAL PIECE OF ADVICE

Before you close this book, let me leave you with the one truth that matters more than any tip or trick I've shared: **Companies don't hire resumes; they hire people.** They're the ones who are:

- **Relentlessly curious.** The ones who ask, "What if we tried this?" instead of just, "What do you need me to do?" They're the ones who see a problem and start digging, not because they were told to, but because they can't help it.

- **Deeply resilient.** The ones who treat a 'no' not as a final judgment, but as the fuel to get smarter for the next 'yes.' They understand that failure isn't a verdict on their worth; it's just a step in the process of learning and growing.

This playbook and insider knowledge is your map and toolkit. Your drive is your most valuable asset, the engine of your success. My goal was to help you realize the power you already possess.

So, go out there with confidence. Be the detective who uncovers the real problems. Be the storyteller who makes the recruiter believe in the solution. Your journey is just beginning. Now, go make them remember your name.

All the best,
Julia

MY GRATITUDE

I wouldn't have had a successful career and be able to share my knowledge to help others were it not for the amazing support system that surrounds me. My husband Derek who stayed back to watch the dog when I had a lot of work travel, who puts up with my crazy ideas (like writing a book and starting a company). My industry friends and family who have supported me through the ups and downs of my career, the challenges and successes. And all the candidates I have met along the way who continue to remind me how important it is to get the Candidate Experience right.

APPENDIX

COMMON BUSINESS ACRONYMS (EXAMPLES):

- AKA: Also Known As
- ASAP: As Soon As Possible
- ATM: At The Moment
- BRB: Be Right Back
- B2B / B2C: Business-to-Business / Business-to-Consumer
- BTW: By The Way
- COB: Close Of Business (Similar to EOD)
- CRM: Customer Relationship Management
- CSS: Cascading Style Sheet (Common in web development)
- CTA: Call To Action (Common in marketing / sales)
- DNS: Domain Name System (Common in IT)
- EOD / EOW: End Of Day / End Of Week
- EOM: End Of Message (Used in emails)
- EPS: Earnings Per Share (Common in finance)
- ETA: Estimated Time Of Arrival
- FTP: File Transfer Protocol (Common in IT)
- FY: Fiscal Year
- FYI: For Your Information
- HR: Human Resources
- HTTP/HTTPS: HyperText Transfer Protocol (Secure) (Common in IT)
- IAC: In Any Case
- ICYMI: In Case You Missed It
- IDK: I Don't Know
- IM: Instant Messaging
- IMO / IMHO: In My Opinion / In My Humble Opinion
- IP: Internet Protocol (Common in IT)
- IPO: Initial Public Offering (Common in finance)
- IIRC: If I Remember Correctly
- ISP: Internet Service Provider (Common in IT)
- IT: Information Technology
- KPI: Key Performance Indicator
- LAN: Local Area Network (Common in IT)
- LBH: Let's Be Honest
- LET: Leaving Early Today
- LMK: Let Me Know
- LOE: Level of Effort
- MOM: Month Over Month (Common in finance / analysis)
- N/A: Not Applicable

- NBD: No Big Deal
- NRN: No Reply Necessary
- NSFW: Not Safe For Work
- NWR: Not Work Related
- OMW: On My Way
- OOO: Out Of Office
- OS: Operating System (Common in IT)
- P&L: Profit and Loss (Common in finance)
- PA: Personal Assistant
- POC: Point of Contact OR Proof of Concept (context matters!)
- PR: Public Relations
- PTE: Part-Time Employee
- QA: Quality Assurance
- QoQ: Quarter over Quarter (Used in Analytics)
- QC: Quality Control
- R&D: Research & Development
- RADAR: Radio Detection and Ranging (Example of an acronym becoming a word)
- Re: Referring to (Used in email subject lines)
- RFD: Request For Discussion
- ROA: Return On Assets (Common in finance)
- ROI: Return On Investment
- RSVP: Please Respond (From French 'Répondez s'il vous plaît')
- RT: Retweet (Common in social media / marketing)
- SaaS: Software as a Service (Common in IT / business)
- SEO: Search Engine Optimization (Common in marketing)
- SM: Social Media (Common in marketing)
- SMB / SME: Small to Medium Business / Small to Medium Enterprise
- SME: Subject Matter Expert
- SOP: Standard Operating Procedure
- SWOT: Strengths, Weaknesses, Opportunities, Threats (Common in business analysis)
- TBD: To Be Decided
- TBH: To Be Honest
- TGIF: Thank God It's Friday
- TIA: Thanks In Advance
- TL;DR / TLTR: Too Long, Didn't Read / Too Long To Read
- TMI: Too Much Information
- TOS: Terms Of Service
- TYT: Take Your Time
- UI: User Interface (Common in IT / design)
- UX: User Experience (Common in IT / design)
- VPN: Virtual Private Network (Common in IT)
- WBS: Work Breakdown Structure
- WDYT: What Do You Think?
- WFH: Work From Home
- WOM / WOMM: Word Of Mouth / Word Of Mouth Marketing

- WYSIWYG: What You See Is What You Get (Common in IT / design)
- XML: Extensible Markup Language (Common in IT)
- YOY: Year Over Year (Common in finance / analysis)
- YTD / MTD: Year To Date / Month To Date (Common in finance / analysis)

www.ingramcontent.com/pod-product-compliance
Lightning Source LLC
Chambersburg PA
CBHW060126130626

46556CB00006B/2252